RC 445 P33

Parker
Mental health
in-service training.

DATE DUE

9/21/76			
MY 03 '78			
AG 25 '82			

LIBRARY
CALIFORNIA SCHOOL OF
PROFESSIONAL PSYCHOLOGY - FRESNO

RC 445 P33

QJ6P

MENTAL HEALTH
IN-SERVICE TRAINING

MENTAL HEALTH IN-SERVICE TRAINING

Some Practical Guidelines
for the Psychiatric Consultant

BEULAH PARKER, M.D.

INTERNATIONAL UNIVERSITIES PRESS, INC.
NEW YORK   NEW YORK

Copyright 1968, by International Universities Press, Inc.
Library of Congress Catalog Card Number: 68-26388

Manufactured in the United States of America

to H. L. V.

CONTENTS

CHAPTER I
Historical Development of an Early In-Service Training Program 1

CHAPTER II
General Comments on In-Service Training 11

CHAPTER III
The Mental Health Consultant as Leader of In-Service Training 20

CHAPTER IV
Shared Attitudes of Workers in Three Professions 42

CHAPTER V
Environmental Sources of Interpersonal Stress 78

CHAPTER VI
Analysis of an In-Service Training Program for Public Health Nurses 94

CHAPTER VII
Analysis of In-Service Training Sessions with Nursery School Personnel 114

CHAPTER VIII
Summary 129

REFERENCES 132

CHAPTER I

HISTORICAL DEVELOPMENT OF AN EARLY IN-SERVICE TRAINING PROGRAM

In 1945, shortly after the close of World War II, the community psychiatry movement had not yet gained momentum. Planners for mental health were still thinking largely in terms of providing more therapeutic facilities for disturbed people, and "prevention of mental illness" to most people still implied the development of child guidance clinics where emotional and behavior problems could be treated at an early stage and parents counseled about healthy child-rearing practices. A few far-sighted professional people in various disciplines were, however, already beginning to realize that treatment facilities alone would never meet the expanding need, not only because of the large number of people needing help, but because an overwhelming proportion of people with emotional troubles and "unhealthy" attitudes would not seek psychotherapeutic help. Dr. Paul Lemkau in Baltimore had instituted psychiatric consultation for public health nurses and was shortly to publish *Mental Hygiene in Public Health* (Lemkau, 1949). In New York, the health department under leadership of Dr. Leona Baumgartner had a similar program, and Dr. Gerald Caplan in Boston was developing facilities for training psychiatrists and others to consult with personnel in various types of community agency. Drs. Milton Senn,

Benjamin Spock, and David Levy, to name only a few, were among those who appreciated the important role pediatricians could play in helping parents avoid training practices which might "cause" neurotic reactions on the part of children. A program of "anticipatory guidance" for parents of children attending well-baby clinics, directed by Dr. J. Levy, was training pediatricians along this line in Newark, N. J. All these programs were relatively new and little known among the vast majority of professional people in psychiatry and public health.

In Berkeley, Calif., a group of community leaders had long been pressing for the establishment of child guidance facilities within the city health department. However, city officials were dedicated to a philosophy shared by most physicians that public health should concentrate on prophylaxis rather than therapy and that direct psychiatric service to patients is not the function of a health department. A committee of consultants from all over the United States was called in to evaluate the local situation and finally recommended that psychiatric consultation be offered to assist health department staff members, primarily those working with parents and children. This would allow workers in direct contact with members of the community to promote the cause of mental health by exercising their own professional skills rather than by attempting to engage in psychotherapy. It was felt that such workers, who deal with people under all sorts of conditions and already enjoy their confidence, might be an important factor in seeing that a person in trouble gets the kind of help needed at the moment. Increased ability to recognize emotional problems, the committee concluded, might enable personnel to prepare people for more successful referral to psychiatric facilities or to forestall the need for referral by preventing the development of the overwhelming anxiety through wiser handling of immediate crises. In January, 1947, on the basis of this recommendation, Dr. Frank

Kelly of the Berkeley City Health Department employed a half-time psychiatric consultant.

The health officer's interest in his new mental health program never flagged, and during the first year he gave valuable cooperation to the consultant in setting up a tentative plan for operations. In the summer of 1948, he participated in an institute on Mental Health in Public Health, jointly sponsored by the California State Department of Public Health and the Commonwealth Fund, which met at the Claremont Hotel in Berkeley. A distinguished faculty of professional people including eight psychiatrists, three pediatricians with psychiatric training, and five public health leaders worked intensively for two weeks with the group of health officers, attempting to give them a new view of public health's potential role in human relations. This venture, the first of its kind, was written up and published as "Public Health is People" by Ethel L. Ginsberg (1950). It proved a great inspiration both to Dr. Kelly and his newly appointed psychiatric consultant who attended the formal teaching sessions. From then on, the inexperienced consultant had an even more unhampered opportunity to experiment flexibly with developing a new program in a relatively new field.

The Berkeley City Health Department acts partly as a teaching facility at the University of California's School of Public Health. In 1947 it served a population of slightly over 110,000 people, sharing operation of a unified public health nursing service with the Berkeley Unified School District and the Visiting Nurse Association. Nurses received part of their salary from each of these agencies. Their duties included helping to control communicable disease and conducting well-child conferences, and they also acted as school nurses and bedside visiting nurses in each district. One of their duties was to deliver the birth certificate of every child born in Berkeley. Each nurse was, therefore, known and trusted by a large segment of the population in her section of the city—not only in the lower-class areas, where public health nurses have always had great influence, but in the middle districts, which housed a large temporarily low-income student population, and in the upper-middle-class "hill districts," where medical and nursing services were for the most part privately financed.

Parent-participating nursery schools, each led by a trained nursery school teacher, were also conducted under administration of the Unified School District and were available to any mother enrolled in an adult education class on preschool education. Three day care centers for the children of working mothers, at that time financed each year by a special appropriation of the state legislature, were administered from an office located in the administration building of the public school system, the administrator working in close cooperation with the head of the parent-participating nursery school program.

Prenatal classes were conducted by Health Department nurses under the auspices of the Visiting Nurse Association, using material compiled by the city department. (Not long afterward, these classes passed out of the Berkeley department's jurisdiction.)

The underlying philosophy was that the principles of mental health should be taught primarily to groups that work with children, either as parents or in professional capacity; the first year's psychiatric consultation program was devised to instruct these groups in matters pertaining to emotional health and disturbance. The program consisted of:

1. Orientation lectures, for public health nurses, on the dynamics of psychosexual development. These explained why certain aspects of child-rearing are important in emotional growth and were intended to make nurses more effective in counseling parents. The lectures were delivered in simple, nontechnical language.

2. Lectures and discussion groups with nurses and

parents in the prenatal classes, stressing the same points.

3. A monthly luncheon meeting with teachers from the parent-participating nursery schools. Material, also somewhat didactically handled, was given to explain the theory and dynamics involved in problems of various children presented by teachers for discussion.

4. A well-child conference, conducted by the consultant (who had also been trained as a pediatrician). This was a small clinic, set up primarily for teaching, where time was available not only to offer the usual instructions on physical care and feeding but also to educate parents about the problems of normal developmental stages and advise them about child-training procedures. Nurses were rotated through this clinic and given an opportunity to see the use of psychoanalytic principles in ordinary pediatric practice. After each clinic, doctor and nurse discussed the cases they had seen.

5. A small counseling service, intended primarily as a teaching instrument for referring personnel. Parents of children with "psychological problems" encountered by nurses or teachers were given guidance interviews. The factors involved in these disturbances were discussed with the referring staff member insofar as this could be done without violating the parents' confidence.[1]

There were many reasons for abandoning most of this approach, but in brief, it became increasingly evident that neither didactic teaching nor direct therapeutic service made the best use of limited psychiatric consultation time. What is more, the latter particularly was creating new problems and new frustrations for the workers.

Every patient or pupil with an emotional symptom of any kind began to be referred to the psychiatrist. Despite explicit exhortations to the contrary, workers felt that either they ought to be doing some form of psychotherapy

[1] A condensed description of the Berkeley program was first published in *California's Health,* January, 1952.

or that any deviant behavior must immediately be referred to an "expert." When they began to understand the dynamics of behavior, cases which they had been handling successfully for years suddenly looked like problems and made them anxious. As they recognized the possible value of psychotherapy to certain people, they lost confidence in the ability to be of service in their own roles. In fact, their reactions were exactly opposite to what had been hoped for and expected. The "emotional problem" began to be seen as an entity in itself rather than as the reaction of a human being within a certain environment under certain conditions. Part of this paradoxical reaction of workers may have been due to the inexperience of the psychiatric consultant, but in retrospect I feel that to a much greater extent it was due to the content-oriented method which was then, and still is, widely used for teaching psychological principles to professional workers who are not psychologically oriented. Even though much of the material interested the staff, it was indigestible.

Many workers lost sight of the fact that with a little insight into mental mechanisms and the emotional needs of children and adults, they themselves could be of great value in protecting and promoting mental health just by doing their own jobs well, and that even when a patient was disturbed enough to need psychotherapy, the cooperation of a wise teacher or family confidant such as a nurse could be an important adjunct to treatment. It seemed important to shift emphasis in the training program toward making staff members feel more effective and bolstering their sense of professional self-esteem by pointing up the value of their own work in creating emotional security among their patients and pupils.

To this end, the consultant spent several months accompanying nurses on their home visits, partly to learn more about the nature of their work, and partly to estimate the

AN EARLY IN-SERVICE TRAINING PROGRAM

value of on-the-spot consultation for workers faced with important decisions in the field.

A difficult case involving emotional disturbance, which was successfully handled by a nurse after a little discussion with the consultant, convinced all health department personnel that a change in the form of the mental health teaching could be of use to them in their own jobs.

Nurse and consultant together visited the home of an eighteen-year-old Italian Catholic girl, happily married and enthusiastic about starting a family, who had just given birth to a boy hideously deformed by vascular anomaly of the head. In addition to being highly unsightly, the lesion was friable and so difficult to dress that no member of the family dared touch it. The mother had become hysterical when she first saw the child; and despite stern admonishment by the family physician that it was her duty to love her son, she had turned her face to the wall, refused to see the priest, and seemed resigned to accepting the feeling of guilt imposed on her both by the doctor and by her peasant grandmother, who insisted that the child had been marked as a result of her own sins. At the time of our visit, the girl was withdrawn and unresponsive. The whole household was tense with anxiety.

Nurse and consultant discussed the psychological factors which might enter into such a reaction and laid out a tentative plan for handling of the case. On her next visit, the nurse calmly assured the young mother that anyone might feel as she did and said that although some people still believed the superstitions about marking children, most professional people felt them to be untrue. She made no effort to persuade the girl to participate in doing the dressings. Coming daily for a number of weeks, she taught the girl's mother how to care for the lesions and talked acceptingly to the still-unresponsive patient about her feelings. After quite a long time, the young mother spontaneously said she might like to hold the child if the nurse would stand by to see that she did not hurt him. Still later, she undertook to do a simple dressing. Gradually her disgust turned to pity for the infant, normal maternal feelings emerged, and she finally accepted full care of the child on her own initiative.

This mother maintained contact with the nurse, who gave practical assistance at many moments of crisis during the following years in which her child underwent repeated plastic surgery operations. For a long time the girl refused to consider having another baby, but with continued acceptance of her feelings and reassurance by someone who had by now become a valuable friend and counselor, she eventually overcame her fears. A normal girl child was born when the boy was seven, and with the nurse's guidance, the mother was able to provide her son with emotional support through the sibling's infancy. Mother and son had developed a close relationship and, when last heard of 10 years after the nurse's original contact, the boy was getting along well in school, had made a satisfactory adjustment to his peer group, and did not seem unduly disturbed by the deformity of extensive scarring.

A successful outcome to the earliest phase of this case gave graphic demonstration that some simple instruction about the nature of guilt reactions enabled the nurse to perform an important psychotherapeutic task merely by carrying out her ordinary nursing function in a nonjudgmental way. The consultant announced that henceforth in-service training sessions would be devoted to helping workers understand the factors that caused interference with their own tasks and that teaching would be based on concrete situations as they arose. For the next 10 years, consultation time was spent in small discussion groups with nurses, nursery school teachers, and the entire staff of each day care center. Each group met approximately once a month, excluding summer vacations. The situation was explicitly structured to offer opportunity for free discussion of any material, on any level, that the workers wished. Subject matter was not limited to emotional problems but would cover any aspect of the workers' jobs that troubled them or any topic related to people and their ways of functioning which interested them. When it seemed appropriate, and when the group climate seemed right, workers would be encouraged to discuss their own reactions and anxieties in relation to problems encountered. However, it was explicitly stated at the outset of the program, and frequently reiterated, that they were not required to expose personal problems to their co-workers and that they need only consider discussing their own reactions when they felt perfectly comfortable in doing so. Any such discussion could be stopped at any time, without explanation, at the request of any worker in the group. Although stress was laid upon the idea that examination of a subject by the group itself would have more ultimate value to workers than didactic teaching, the consultant would occasionally respond to requests for lectures on topics of immediate concern to the whole group and would occasionally suggest topics for discussion if at any particular time a group had no ideas of its own.

The public health nursing staff preferred to hold separate sessions for workers and supervisors, believing, I think rightly, that both groups would feel freer to express themselves in the absence of personnel from another administrative level. At meetings of nursery school and day care personnel, the overall program administrators were sometimes present, but frequently they remained absent to give staff members an opportunity to discuss ideas and feelings that might not come out in the presence of someone with the authority to evaluate their performance.

After this method of conducting discussions had been in

operation for several years, a questionnaire asking for comments and suggestions was given to the public health nurses, who filled it out anonymously and returned it to their supervisor for relay to the consultant. Although one individual stated that she had found the discussions a waste of time and another said she had resented "being psychoanalyzed," members of the group almost unanimously reported that they felt their effectiveness with patients had been improved. Many stated specifically that they had found most valuable the opportunity to understand their own reactions and those of their patients. Similar reports were obtained from the nursery school group. In short, these workers subscribed wholeheartedly to a concept of task-oriented in-service training which is the subject of this book.

CHAPTER II

GENERAL COMMENTS ON IN-SERVICE TRAINING

THE NEED

Within the last few years as never before, large numbers of people in the United States have become aware of the need to improve mental health and social functioning throughout all levels of society. Increasing emphasis on the importance of community psychiatry also demonstrates growing recognition within the psychotherapeutic professions themselves that many attacks on the spreading problem of emotional disturbance will have to be made through workers in community facilities that are not designated as specifically therapeutic. Experimentation with diverse ways of promoting mental health in elements of the population that either cannot or will not make use of individual or group psychotherapy is now taking place on a wide scale.

Workers in many professions encounter people in all walks of life who exhibit glaring signs of emotional instability or who show evidence of less obvious problems through their inability to make good use of the services they seek. Sometimes a worker, although not aware that his client has emotional problems, finds his own task impeded by the fact that a client makes unreasonable responses to reasonable suggestions or cannot establish an adequate working relationship with the one who is trying to help him. Such frustrating confrontation is the daily fare for many members of the so-called "helping professions," welfare workers, health department personnel, nursery school personnel and public school teachers.

Members of these nonpsychotherapeutic helping professions can be significant figures in the community psychiatry movement. They can play a vital role in furthering the mental health of their clients or pupils by helping them find effective ways of resolving immediate conflict situations in important areas of their lives, often at periods of greatest susceptibility to change, and in so doing, lay the groundwork for more effective patterns of functioning in general. However, members of such professions often have received very little education about mental health or illness or about factors involved in irrational actions and reactions by presumably "normal" people. Although many professional schools for these groups of workers have recently shown some tendency to introduce courses on developmental psychology and behavioral science, such courses are for the most part minor parts of the curriculum. They have tended to stress abstract theory and often have proved grossly inadequate as practical tools for a worker to use with confidence when face to face with actual human beings in distress, acting in unaccountable ways. An ever-increasing number of agencies, institutions, and groups of professional workers themselves are therefore seeking supplementary teaching based on the experiences of workers under the conditions of their particular jobs.

National planners for mental health are taking cognizance of the potential value of teaching programs for workers already on the job and are encouraging the use of federal and local mental health funds to set up in-service training for groups of workers on the staffs of many agencies and institutions who deal in different capacities either with people at crucial developmental periods of their lives or those who are for one reason or another in need or in trouble. Through specialized professional assistance, these workers are given basic education in psychodynamic principles, personality development and behavioral patterns and are helped to improve their own effectiveness by application of these principles to their work problems.

PREVALENT APPROACHES TO IN-SERVICE TRAINING

An in-service training program is usually set up in accordance with one of three basic philosophies for working with members of professions not specifically oriented to psychological concepts. These approaches may be characterized as worker-centered, client- or content-centered, or task-centered. Each has fervent adherents. The first two will be mentioned only briefly, without delineating their concepts in detail.

The worker-centered approach is not to be confused with a method described by Caplan as "consultee-centered consultation," which takes place on a one-to-one basis. That term applies to situations where a personal conflict theme from the worker's own life, which has intruded upon his ability to perceive the client's problem, is recognized by the consultant and handled by a discussion of the client's problem in a way that is also indirectly therapeutic to the worker, although personal reasons for the worker's conflict are not discussed (Caplan, 1964). I refer to an approach based on the belief that a leader of in-service training groups can best teach about general patterns of emotional expression and behavior by making members of the worker group conscious of their *own* emotional processes and ways of interacting with him and with other members of the group. They will then presumably function better in all their interpersonal relationships and will be better able to understand the emotional reactions and motivations of their clients. Group discussion focuses almost exclusively upon the worker's own feelings about his job problems and about his clients.

There are a number of variations of this approach. It is particularly popular with certain psychiatrists who have been trained to conduct even the supervision of trainees in the psychological professions as a form of therapy. In my opinion, use of this approach with psychologically unsophisticated worker groups carries certain dangers. First and foremost, even though a program leader explicitly states his intention to operate in this way from the beginning, and a group voices no resistance, members of the group frequently experience enough anxiety and latent antagonism to prevent much real learning. The vast majority of psychologically unsophisticated workers feel that their privacy is violated by a demand to expose personal reactions and defenses in a group of colleagues with whom they must be in daily contact and resent the implication that they themselves will be a major subject for discussion. A high-morale group, within the framework of a secure relationship to an individual leader, may sometimes elect to explore their own reactions to certain kinds of problems. When this occurs voluntarily in a climate of explicit readiness, it has a very different impact than it would when undertaken routinely without regard for the character of a particular group. Second, it is only occasionally sufficient to meet worker's needs. Although emotional reactions and interpersonal problems play a significant part in the work difficulties of most professional people, those who lack specific psychological training may also lack basic information about mental health and illness. Such information, which can be extremely helpful in understanding certain kinds of work difficulties, does not usually emerge from discussions focused on their own reactions.

The client-and-content-centered approach is time-honored and widely adopted. Case material, prepared and presented to the group by a worker, is focused largely on the behavior of a client, patient, or pupil and on the factors underlying his emotional reactions. Discussions and lectures on abstract principles of mental functioning are also conducted by the program leader in a hope that workers will later be able to use such knowledge in understanding the motivations of other cases as well. Adherents to this philosophy view in-service training as an extension of basic professional education. They avoid the pitfall of making a teaching group into something akin to group therapy and seldom create incapacitating anxiety in a group. Workers may receive useful information and are often considerably gratified by exposure to the theoretical concepts of a field which elicits widespread interest among educated people. However, the impact of material presented in this way may remain relatively superficial.

Most people are best motivated to learn concepts which have a personal meaning to them and find abstract theoretical principles most useful when related to their own concrete experience. A professional worker's interest in the mental and emotional processes of a client is greatest when knowledge about the client throws light on a *specific interaction* between him and the worker or on some aspect of the client's behavior which has been interfering with the worker's ability to accomplish his own professional goal. General discussions related to *other* aspects of the client's experience may have only academic interest to a professional person whose primary concern is to carry out a particular transaction. The worker's task may not require extensive knowledge of the client's developmental history or patterns of typical reaction. It *may* require an understanding of particular conditions which prevent the client from participating in some procedure designed to help him. Most workers want from in-service training an experience that will improve their own professional performance, and they tend to absorb most effectively only ideas that apply to the work problem facing them at any particular time. Subject matter unrelated to their own specific task frequently cannot be properly digested and integrated with the body of professional knowledge they already possess.

A task-centered approach is the one I consider most efficient. Proponents assume that in-service training for professional workers who are not psychologically oriented is best accomplished by stressing factors that may be interfering with a worker's ability to carry out a *specific* aspect of his professional role with a *particular* client under *particular* conditions. The group leader must evaluate a worker's interaction with his client in its total framework, discern the sources of the worker's difficulty with this particular person at this particular time, and use his own professional skills to help break the block to a successful completion of the worker's task. He adopts whatever focus is appropriate to a particular situation and flexibly adapts his method of operation to the immediate need.

The worker's job may be impeded almost entirely by factors that lie within the psychic structure of the client. Certain kinds of abnormality or defensive operation can defeat even the most skillful worker's effort to make meaningful contact. Or the problem may lie in a worker's inability to handle the forces with which he is dealing, through either the lack of experience in use of his professional skills or the lack of education in recognizing specific forms of psychopathology and covert ways of expressing affect. He may have taken a client's defensive hostility at face value or failed to appreciate hostility veiled by overtly compliant behavior. In such cases, the leader may be required only to give information about the client's reactions in order to reduce the worker's anxiety and give him the tools with which to improve his own function in the client's behalf.

One example is the case of a public health nurse who described a problem she had answering a patient's questions. The mother of a newborn child with a cleft palate had studied about psychological development and believed that a child makes the best adjustment to the birth of a sibling at two years. Now her first child had been born with a defect which the surgeon said should be repaired by major operation at the age of two. Would it be better for him if she had the baby sooner and risked having this child operated upon at the height of sibling rivalry, or should she plan to have the next baby on schedule, just at the time this one was having major surgery?

Here the problem was obviously one of anxiety and ambivalence in the mother, causing her to be concerned with birth of a second child before her first was yet three days old. When the group leader pointed out the universality of ambivalence in parents with defective children, discussing the unconscious guilt and overcompensatory concern which prompted this mother to move away from one baby to the next, the group saw her questions in a new light. Without further help, the nurse herself was able to find ways to relieve the mother's guilt for her disappointment and to help her accept the need to defer all decisions about the child's future.

On the other hand, the worker's own emotional reactions may have interfered with his objectivity toward a client's problem. Such reactions frequently arise from transference and displacement, set in motion by a specific type of client; they may also occur in response to feelings of anxiety and helplessness aroused by a particular situation or by some conflict between the needs of the client and the needs of a worker in his professional capacity. An understanding of the worker's ways of interacting with people in general may be quite relevant to the immediate problem. He may have lost objectivity through some threat to his sense of security, arising from a variety of sources specific to this one interaction, including the impact of factors in the setting where he and the client come together.

To illustrate how such a situation may occur, I shall describe a discussion which again took place around the case presented by a public health nurse. A querulous old lady was convalescing from a stroke, and although there was now nothing wrong with her physically, she continued to refuse to do anything for herself. This was highly irritating to the nurse who, although she knew better, found herself frequently and somewhat punitively lecturing the old lady about taking a more "positive attitude." Her sympathies were with the husband who seemed to be enslaved. He himself was threatened with blindness, but he was often prevented from keeping his clinic appointments by a need to stay with his wife. The nurse felt unable to cope with the situation because she herself felt antagonistic.

Because this came up in a high-morale group of nurses with a good understanding of psychology, discussion could center around the hostile reaction of the nurse. She soon brought out the fact that there was a dependent member in her own family, causing her to overidentify with the husband. At the same time, she defended her attitude as a universal reaction to a selfish, demanding person and wanted help in learning to like this woman. Everyone in the group, including the leader, agreed that such a person is difficult to like but wondered why the nurse felt called upon to do so in order to handle the situation. At this point someone suggested the possibility of an unconscious wish on the husband's part to become helpless himself. In the course of discussing an interplay of dependency needs between two old people, the nurse suddenly recognized that her own unconscious wish for dependency took part in her conflict of feeling about these patients. Although at first shocked, she received enough reassurance from the group to relieve her anxiety, and she later handled the problem satisfactorily.

Even though a group leader may find it advisable to help provide insight into a worker's own sources of conflict, he should always do so in reference to the specific task that the worker is trying to carry out with a particular client in a particular setting.

CHAPTER III

THE MENTAL HEALTH CONSULTANT AS LEADER OF IN-SERVICE TRAINING

As in-service training programs proliferate in many types of agencies and institutions, psychiatrists are being employed as consultants to lead them, along with a few specifically trained clinical psychologists and psychiatric social workers. Many people would like to reserve the term "consultant" for one who carries out a well-defined process, conceptualized and distinguished from other forms of training activity by Caplan (1964). In general usage, however, the title "mental health consultant" is apt to fall on anyone trained in the theories and techniques of psychiatry, psychology, or psychoanalysis who is employed to apply his specialized knowledge and skills to the problems encountered by workers who are not trained in psychology.

Although many skilled mental health consultants in the United States today have acquired extensive experience with techniques of in-service teaching during the gradual development of this field over the past 25 years, few of them are available to the average community facility faced with a prospect of setting up such a program for the first time. Facilities for training members of the psychological professions specifically for mental health consultation are still limited to a few professional training centers, which have, to date, a relatively small number of graduates. Although such training will undoubtedly expand rapidly, most psychiatrists now employed to conduct in-service training at agencies or institutions such as public schools are new to this kind of activity, even though they may have had extensive experience in the practice of psychoanalysis or psychotherapy and supervised or consulted with psychiatric residents and social workers in therapeutic clinics and family service agencies. The same may be said of clinical psychologists and psychiatric social workers skilled in their own professional disciplines but unacquainted with a consultant's role. Many are from the ranks of younger members in their own professions, not yet secure enough with the techniques of their own fields to have great assurance in using their knowledge of psychodynamics in other ways. They may be experienced in group *therapy* techniques, but usually they have had little opportunity during their training to acquire skills in handling discussions in a "normal" group. Most will themselves be learning on the job and proceeding more or less by trial and error. Supervision in acquiring new professional skills, although highly desirable (Parker, 1961), may not be available in many communities.

When a mental health consultant, new to his role, comes to an agency adopting in-service training for the first time, his choice of modus operandi is determined not only by factors existing within the individual agency, but also by attitudes of his own derived from previous modes of professional functioning. In the following material I shall attempt to point out some areas where it may be useful for him to examine his own attitudes and those of others before planning a method of handling a particular group. Although I shall point out a few situations that may be encountered, no attempts will be made to give concrete advice on handling, since each therapist has his own style and will have to evaluate immediate situations in his own way.

INFLUENCES ON INITIAL METHODS OF OPERATION

Bias arising from previous training and experience as a psychotherapist may to some extent complicate a consultant's ability to assume the role of leader in an in-service training group. When working with an individual, the therapist's role is to focus on the intrapsychic problems of that one person. He must understand the patient and help improve his relationships with others, but the therapist's primary responsibility is to the patient himself and not to others in his external environment, except under extreme conditions. In a one-to-one therapeutic relationship, it is also explicitly recognized by both members that the patient must verbalize personal feelings and reactions in order to perform the therapeutic task. A therapist values a patient with the capacity for self-awareness and may gauge treatability by the degree to which a patient is willing and able to recognize the nature of his involvements with others.

When he undertakes in-service training, the therapist undergoes a basic change in role. He now must keep in mind the needs of several people—the *client* brought up for discussion, the *discussing group* as an entity, and *individual members* of that group. He must maintain a basic therapeutic attitude and be aware of sources for individual anxiety, but his focus must now be on the *task* of discussion group members. He must consider as of primary importance not only the impact of a disturbed client on the environment in which he functions with a worker but also the impact of discussing psychological disturbance with a group of workers who have not been desensitized to instinctual material. There is also .a change in the explicit and implicit contract between therapist and discussants concerning the desirability of verbalizing personal feelings and recognizing personal involvements. Behavior and attitudes valued in a therapeutic relationship, and considered "normal" to it, may actually be deviant in a different kind of interaction.

For example, a research-minded young psychiatrist, embarking on in-service training with groups of elementary school teachers, considered as "normal" the behavior of one group out of six which accepted preliminary psychological testing for themselves without protest; he looked for "pathology" of individual members to explain the discomfort shown by a group of older educators during a highly unstructured discussion. Actually, teachers who failed to resist the idea of having their *own* psyches explored by an unknown consultant were denying by intellectualization an initial anxiety that is universal among groups that are not psychologically oriented during their first contact with a psychiatrist. If older members of a profession predominantly accustomed to didactic and content-oriented discussions had been completely comfortable from the outset in an unstructured group led by a psychiatrist, they too would have been reacting abnormally.

Long-standing interest in disturbed individuals may cause the mental health consultant for groups of professional workers consciously or unconsciously to focus on the needs of the troubled client rather than on the needs and conflicts of those who are trying to deal with him in an agency setting. When, for instance, a teacher presents for discussion the case of a disturbed child, a therapist may stress how valuable a teacher may be in meeting a child's need, losing sight of the fact that a teacher has primary professional responsibility to a whole group whose interests might have to be sacrificed by concentration on one individual.

Assumption of a new role in itself generates the anxiety and insecurity customarily experienced by any student or trainee. Even though he may have had many years of successful experience in his own field, a therapist who for the first time undertakes in-service training for personnel of psychologically unsophisticated professions is again "on the spot" to show aptitude for learning and for applying knowledge in a new way. What is more, a clinically trained person willing to give professional time for this purpose usually has some sense of dedication to the importance of community psychiatry and feels a responsibility to convince administrators of his agency that such a program will fulfill their hopes for improving the function of both workers and clients and for meeting a need in the community which supports it. As respresentative of the mental health professions to professional people hitherto largely unacquainted with anyone from a field regarded as alien and threatening, he may also feel a personal responsibility to be liked as well as to be useful. Anyone who for any reason snows hostility, resistance, or disapproval may threaten his feelings of competence, no matter how well he has learned to understand and handle such attitudes on the part of psychotherapy patients. The anxiety aroused may create blocks which affect the way he carries out his role. For instance, a psychiatrist trainee at a Community Psychiatry Training Center, conducting in-service training with groups of school teachers, reacted to covert hostility and competitiveness on the part of a school psychologist by failing to notice the numerous ways in which the psychologist sabotaged plans made jointly by the teachers, the psychiatrist, and the overtly cooperative psychologist himself. The consultant trainee could not understand reasons for the groups' increasing frustration, although the psychologist's part in impeding constructive action was glaringly obvious to the trainee's supervisor.

Attitudes prevalent within the agency by which he is employed also influence the therapist's initial activities. Most agencies setting up such a program for the first time have a specific set of preexisting expectations and felt needs, determined by a combination of realistic conditions in the agency setting and more subtle factors which often constitute potent hidden sources of positive and negative motivation for learning a new kind of material. These expectations and needs will to some extent affect the way a new consultant must function before he gains the confidence of workers.

The individual character of an agency has influence upon the kind of teaching program that can initially be set up and the way it can be carried out. Although one may speak in general about optimal ways for a consultant to function in a mental health in-service training program for a particular type of worker, every agency or institution has a specific atmosphere which will determine the kind of focus that its staff can best utilize at any given time.

I shall take as example a single public school in any community. Many theories have been proposed to define the best methods of training teachers for children of the elementary grade levels to understand and meet the emotional needs of their pupils. In actual fact, however, there is no one method that will be universally successful. Every school has its own set of internal conditions to which any plan for teacher training must be flexibly adapted if it is to be really successful in modifying teacher attitudes. These conditions may vary greatly from those existing even in another school of the same type serving the same kind of population area in the same town. Although the nature of the work and previous training of the teachers is roughly the same, variations in the pressures acting upon teachers in their immediate setting will influence not only the kind of program they can accept but also the degree to which they may be expected to benefit from it and pass the benefits on to their pupils. A most important influence creating differences in the climates of various schools is the attitude of individual principals.

In any school, the principal is supposedly undisputed leader, endowed by the higher administration with considerable autonomy in carrying out the overall policies of the school system. He is also exposed to varying pressures from outside and inside his own organization which often have a strong influence upon the way he runs his school. Every school is therefore to some degree individual in its operation, depending on its leadership and the nature of pressures on it.

As I stated earlier, many national and local leaders promoting the cause of community mental health endorse the value of in-service training for teachers, and a particular school board or superintendent may respond to public opinion by urging the introduction of such a program into their school system. An individual principal may agree to follow the general trend, supported by a bloc of young teachers with "modern" ideas and backed by an "enlightened" segment of the larger community. At the same time, a strong group of older teachers, well-known and respected by parents of the district and supported by more conservative forces, may consider such a program an unnecessary burden added to an already crushing work load. Intrastaff tensions thus created may affect the efficiency of the school as a whole, and be reflected in attitudes of the wider community toward the school and its operation. This may enhance the ambivalence which the principal may already feel toward his new program. He may wish to accept a concept approved by many distinguished educators, yet he may share a fear that is exceedingly common among educational administrators that a consultant from outside the field of public education might influence the attitudes of his teachers and undermine the traditional status of school authorities. Regardless of whether he has given his consent to the operation of an in-service training program in his school, the principal's reaction to intramural and extramural politics, as well as many factors within his own personality, will determine whether he subtly encourages or discourages teachers from making use of the new ideas to which they are being given access. The actual intraschool power structure and the various intrapsychic and interpersonal forces playing upon a principal are never the same in any two schools, but the principal's attitude is a vital factor in success or failure of any program designed to involve teachers under his authority. Although a consultant in charge of setting up in-service training for the school system as a whole may have a general plan for the way he wants to function, this plan often will have to be considerably modified according to the expectations and felt needs of members in a hierarchy at any individual school. Before making any definite plan of operation, he will have to evaluate the climate at each individual school and try to determine which procedure is least likely to encounter overt or subtle resistance from those who are in power. Sometimes this takes quite a while.

One may say the same about any health or welfare agency. Variations in the way the power structure functions and the influence of important personalities responsible for carrying out administrative policies affect the character of the agency and have an important impact upon the workers within it and upon the ways in which they will react to any form of in-service training.

In any type of agency, workers will also have toward a mental health consultant certain expectations based on pre-existent and often stereotyped ideas held by their profession as a whole toward members of the consultant's profession as a whole. Traditional status relationships and traditional ways in which members of one profession have worked with members of the other will have some effect on the kind of working relationship that can initially be established between a consultant and any group of workers. Patterns of behavior between members of the respective professions have a deep historical base, as do traditional attitudes of equality or rivalry between various professions, regardless of the ways in which individual members react to each other.

As an example, we may use doctors and nurses. Long-standing tradition has established a great status differential between these two professions. In any discussions between them, it is assumed that a doctor will take the lead and that a nurse is expected to accept his opinions without question. Such an assumption can seldom be modified simply by stating that a different kind of interaction will take place under specific conditions. A consultant from the psychiatric profession, for instance, who plans to set up a program of informal, unstructured discussion with groups of nurses in a health department will find himself confronted by people who believe firmly that doctor-nurse relationships are inevitably carried out overtly or covertly along hierarchical and authoritarian lines. This concept can be changed only gradually, over a fairly long period of time. Even if the doctor repeatedly and consistently demonstrates a nonauthoritarian attitude, the idea may never be erased entirely. No matter how a particular doctor feels about the possibility of mutuality in a relationship with nurses, or what he explicitly tells the nurses about his intentions, generations of nurses have interacted with doctors according to certain patterns which are not readily abandoned. Implicit demands for authoritative statements of fact and opinion are almost always made by nurses initially in any teaching situation conducted by an M.D. A group leader from the profession of psychiatric nursing or social work, operating with the same nurses, will encounter a different set of implicit demands, based on the different views that nurses hold concerning a relationship between their profession and that of the leader.

As another example, let us take the professions of psychiatry and social work, which are also historically linked in a certain kind of working relationship. For a long time, psychiatrists have been called upon to act as consultants to certain social agencies. For the most part, workers within these agencies have themselves been fairly well-trained in theories and skills of psychotherapy, and group consultations have generally been conducted through presentations of formalized case material, prepared in advance by the worker, with discussions based on patient psychodynamics. Many agency workers have come to expect this kind of interaction with a psychiatric consultant. In recent years, however, some attempts have been made to develop in-service training programs for public welfare agencies where many workers, although confronted by clients with overwhelming emotional problems, either are completely untrained or have had minimal opportunity to learn psychodynamic principles or psychotherapeutic techniques in their field placements. When such a program is led by a psychiatrist, he may encounter resistance to change in a method of interaction that has become traditional between members of his profession and social agency consultees. Any attempt to teach psychodynamic principles by focusing on the workers' own task may be seen by workers themselves as threatening, by supervisors as an invasion of their territory, and by agency administrators as a danger to agency traditions and a possible interference with the agency's responsibility to the community. Mental health consultants from other professions will meet other expectations based on their traditional roles or on a lack of familiarity with their qualifications for acting as consultants to a particular type of agency. For instance, although the status of certain psychiatric social workers as consultants to family service agencies has long been assured as being comparable to that of psychiatrists acting in the client-centered way, they may encounter difficulty in having their status recognized by the principal of a school, even though they may be accepted by guidance workers who are also trained social workers. Clinical psychologists may be treated as colleagues by academic personnel even more readily than psychiatrists, but they will be expected to function didactically and will need to demonstrate that less traditional ways of interacting can help workers function more effectively in the interests of their clients. Time may also be needed to help consultants from mental health professions who lack medical training to handle their own feelings when their status is held in question by agency personnel.

The personnel of educational institutions at all grade levels are often largely unacquainted with principles of psychodynamics or the factors which affect mental health and illness. Many individuals within the public school system have read a good deal of psychological literature, and not a few who live in sophisticated urban districts have been exposed to psychoanalysis or therapy for themselves or their friends and relatives. On the whole, however, teachers still tend to share the ignorance and prejudice about such matters which is prevalent in other professions that are not psychologically oriented and in the population at large. Preexisting anxieties about anything to do with "abnormality" and stereotypes about psychologists and psychiatrists will affect the way in-service training can be started if it is directed toward educators themselves rather than toward trained guidance workers within the school faculty.

The existence of immediate need obviously affects a consultant's initial activities. If the introduction of in-service training coincides with or results from some crisis within an agency, the consultant must first find some solution to the acute situation. If he does not, he may add frustration and heightened antagonism to any preexisting ambivalence of workers toward him and thus make the task of gaining their confidence in his own way of working with them difficult or impossible.

The nature of felt need also poses a different kind of demand upon consultants from different disciplines. If, for instance, a worker asks for a medical diagnostic opinion or for suggestions about helping a client with physical disabilities, a medical consultant will feel more pressure to treat the case as strictly a medical problem than consultants from other professions would, particularly if clinical facilities for referral are limited or unavailable in a particular community. Even though he recognizes that an irrational fear of a psychiatrist can induce workers to focus on demands for concrete advice, an M.D. may have to overlook such fears to some extent until he has had time to show the workers that his skill as a mental health consultant can be more valuable to them when directed into other channels. The felt needs of agency workers may differ markedly from what a consultant considers most important to them, but these needs cannot be ignored at the beginning of any training program.

Knowledge of a group's training for their own profession may be a constructive influence on the way a mental health consultant handles certain kinds of material, particularly at the beginning of in-service training. Knowledge about subject matter that has been *stressed* in their professional education may help him to select the most significant aspect of a case discussion for emphasis. A consultant may at times be in a good position to help workers focus on shared sources of anxiety if he understands the technical requirements of their profession and is aware of whether a worker who is having difficulty handling a situation is deviating from methods approved by his own supervisors. To give an example from my own experience as consultant to a group of public health nurses, when a competent nurse had trouble with a patient, the group failed to bring out that she was actually violating a basic nursing tenet. The case and its handling are briefly described in Chapter VI. At a patient's request, a nurse agreed to give unsolicited advice to the patient's neighbor and got into difficulties. Since I was unaware of the degree to which the teaching of public health nursing stresses a need to avoid the very situation she was in, I missed an excellent opportunity to demonstrate that her violation stemmed from a source of anxiety shared by most public health nurses. Discussion of the feelings aroused when nurses are pressured by patients to step outside what they see as their correct professional roles, and the results of those feelings, would have been far more meaningful to the group than any other aspect of the case. As it was, I misdirected the discussion by concentrating on the nurse's immediate problem instead of the general problem.

Knowledge of material that has been *omitted* from the training level of a particular professional group may also give valuable direction to the activity of a group leader. Many consultants assume that all workers are uniformly educated about matters relevant to their own work, not recognizing that there may be a wide spread in the level and quality of professional education not only among members of different generations in any profession but even among individuals of roughly the same age. Any one group of nursery school teachers, for instance, may contain individuals who, although they are experienced in the care of small children, have had almost no formal theoretical training, and others, recently graduated from first-class training centers, who know a lot of theory but less about how to apply it. While one might expect all school teachers to have received some education about the physical and emotional growth stages of children, not all of them have, particularly teachers in the higher grades whose training stresses acquiring knowledge of academic subject matter and teaching it to students. Although it is often assumed that doctors and nurses are fully educated about all matters pertaining to bodily function, curricula of many medical and nursing schools have glaringly omitted reference to the whole area of sexual response and patterns of sexual behavior. A recent graduate of a first-class nursing school told me not long ago that in her anatomy course only rudimentary information was given about the genitalia, and that even this small amount pertained entirely to the female organs. Information about male genitalia was technically included in the course plan, but year after year, "time ran out" before any class got to them. Sexuality, excretion, and deviant ways of expressing instinctual impulse are generally taboo subjects even in the training of workers who will be concerned to a great extent with physical problems of human beings. If professional teachers have discussed these subjects at all, they have often done so in an indirect, evasive way. Serious discussion of these matters in a group of workers has remained a source of anxiety for most nurses, many doctors, and even a considerable number of social welfare workers, who should have had some exposure to these ideas in the course of their training, as well as school teachers and other professional groups. A member of a psychological profession who has become desensitized to discussion of such matters during his own training is not always prepared for such attitudes and may inadvertently antagonize or frighten an unsophisticated group by careless language or premature introduction of shocking concepts.

The nature of his relationship to the agency as a whole may have an important influence on the way a consultant is able to carry out his teaching. A leader detached from intra-agency politics can more readily create an atmosphere where workers will feel able to express their feelings about things in general and about agency policies or persons of authority in particular. If workers know that the consultant has no responsibility to administer, supervise, or evaluate personnel, they will have far greater confidence in his ability to empathize with their insecurities without betraying their inadequacies. In many agencies, the consultant who is a psychiatrist may be asked to advise administrators about the emotional stability of some staff member or members. He may also be asked by supervisors, or even by a worker himself, to "talk things over" with someone who feels or is felt to be under stress. His position as leader of in-service training almost invariably will be damaged by fulfilling such requests. Occasionally an individual staff member may regard refusal of personal counsel as a rejection, but for the most part, workers have no desire for a consultant to become a therapist and may be greatly threatened in their relationship to him if he steps into another role.

Although outside contact between the consultant and discussion group members is often considered undesirable, informal friendly relationship sometimes can help create a relaxed atmosphere, particularly where the staff has little knowledge of mental health concepts. Stereotyped ideas about psychiatrists, for example, are still prevalent enough to warrant an attempt at dissipating them by some degree of social contact if the occasion arises naturally. In schools or health departments, a consultant is frequently invited to join in the celebration of a birthday or some other special occasion. His willingness to participate and break the usual chain-of-command relationship may encourage a climate favorable to the free exchange of ideas which is so essential to his role. Acceptance of any teacher's ideas is always facilitated by acceptance of the teacher himself in a human relationship.

Every in-service training program should be specifically constructed to meet the needs of a particular group. From the foregoing discussion, it will be clear that in order to perform this function most adequately, a consultant must acquire as quickly as possible knowledge about the group with which he will be working, the agency setting in which they operate, the nature of their work and their training for it, and the attitudes and traditional views shared by other members of their profession. Until he has gained such knowledge, he will be wise to remember the virtue of humility and to set a limited goal for his own usefulness.

THE CONSULTANT'S ATTITUDE AND ACTIVITY

In general, the leader of in-service training should be a noncritical, interested coinvestigator of problems raised by the group, providing guidance for its members in the respectful mutual interchange of ideas and experiences. He should attempt to create a nonpunitive, noncoercive group atmosphere where workers can feel confident and undefensive and where, by the use of appropriate techniques, he can stimulate meaningful discussions. Encouraging the interest and voluntary participation of group members, he should attempt to minimize resistances by keeping anxiety low and by respecting personal reticence. With such attitudes, he may expect the initial suspicions and guardedness of group members gradually to diminish.

A consultant should help determine the nature of discussion at each stage by assuming active leadership or by encouraging a group's effort to explore a topic for themselves. His functions, both explicit and implicit, are to give information and to stimulate group thinking, in which he should participate. When appropriate, he should encourage group investigation of emotional reactions that create work difficulties. A more detailed presentation of the ways to conduct a discussion group for professional workers of agencies not specifically therapeutic in purpose will be given in Chapter VI. Here I will only comment briefly on factors which influence his choice of method at any one time.

INFLUENCES UPON A CONSULTANT'S CHOICES OF ACTIVITY

Clinical judgment is the most important influence upon a consultant's activity. In each session, he has to evaluate the nature of a group's stated and underlying problems and form major decisions about what to make explicit and what to handle by implication. Of course, often while one purpose is served explicitly another is advanced implicitly. For instance, when he gives information to a group of workers on psychic mechanisms, syndromes, or disturbances, his explicit goal is to clarify reasons for the behavior of people with whom the workers have come in contact through their jobs; as he demonstrates that the behavior of the patients is not directed at workers personally, he hopes by implication to relieve feelings of anxiety and guilt about their relationships with these people. Similarly, if the consultant gives workers a specific suggestion for managing a situation, he at the same time gives support and helpful information. By citing his own experience in dealing with similar situations, he shares responsibility with the workers and gives the support of "authority" to certain attitudes and procedures. In quoting from relevant literature, he strengthens the workers' confidence in a course of action and relieves emotional pressure. Often his goal is reached more satisfactorily by not being too explicit.

In-service training group members often feel they are a captive audience. Even though participation is "voluntary," many workers attend only because they would feel conspicuous if they did not. Personal dynamics in most groups are therefore exceedingly varied, and in some there may be good reason to avoid exploration of feelings completely. As mentioned earlier, the selection and training of many workers do not stress the need for self-awareness; often it is feared and considered inappropriate. The consultant must use clinical judgment to evaluate the degree of "psychological-mindedness" of individuals within each group and the morale of the entire group, for together these factors determine the group's probable tolerance for examining the emotional reactions of individuals.

Clinical experience is important for estimating anxiety levels in general or in regard to specific types of material, in determining the nature of group interaction, and in estimating the best level and focus for discussion. Only through clinical experience can the consultant know whether to bring covert resistances and hostilities of a group into the open. Often it is best to limit discussion to the case being presented and deal only indirectly with group reactions. Although feelings of this kind are explicitly acknowledged as a focus for investigation in group therapy, airing them in a group of co-workers may be of questionable value. Resistance to exploration of individual reactions is often intensified if workers are pressed in this direction.

One example of this took place during a session in which a young public health nurse presented her dilemma.

After an illness, a kindergarten child had successfully resisted all efforts of both her mother and the school authorities to get her back to school. The nurse felt caught between the teacher, who was insisting on a punitive approach, and the mother, whose feelings about forcing the child to return to school were obviously ambivalent. She did not know how to advise the mother.

Before discussion began, the consultant mentioned that this sounded like a typical example of school phobia and asked the group what more they wanted to know about the situation before attempting to evaluate it. An immediate and heated response came from several nurses, who maintained that such a reaction was extremely common after an illness and that the child would benefit if it were forced to return to school by whatever means could be employed. The psychiatrist commented that although children often welcome a "push" to overcome resistance of this kind, occasionally such a push makes the situation worse. Again the nurses were asked to consider criteria for making a decision about this individual case, but their resistance solidified and nothing emerged from the discussion except further and more heated insistence that the child should be forced back to school.

The consultant then suggested a possibility that since kindergarten children legally do not have to be in school at all, it might be unnecessary to force the issue. The group contended, now violently, that "if the child gets away with this, she will develop a pattern of insisting on her own way." They refused even to consider the child's level of maturity, her previous adjustment to kindergarten, or the circumstances immediately surrounding her refusal to return.

A number of nurses involved in this discussion were known to be in open disagreement with several aspects of health department policy. Although school personnel frequently react to schcol phobias with somewhat irrational intensity, the consultant was fairly certain that the nurses' display of violent feeling against a "rebellious" child represented displacement of their own unconscious guilt for rebellion against authority. When the group was asked why they felt so strongly on the subject, they brushed the question aside.

The consultant then supplied information on factors which may underlie this type of reaction in a child and explained some of the reasons why school personnel in general often feel threatened by school phobias. The nurse who originally presented the case learned some useful facts and, realizing that some of her original feeling of helplessness had resulted from intimidation by the teacher, felt more competent to talk with the mother. The rest of the group expressed a feeling that they had learned some interesting theoretical material about school phobias and adjourned on a friendly note.

The same case presented to several other groups brought no duplication of the first group's violent reaction, although a feeling of anxiety about successful defiance of authority was detectable in all. This seemed to confirm the consultant's opinion that the reaction had resulted from threatening intrapsychic conflicts peculiar to individual members of the first group. Exploration and discussion of those personal conflicts would not have been appropriate for any in-service training group and would have been disastrous for this particular group.

On the other hand, there are times when it *is* appropriate to discuss the relationship between a worker's emotional reaction and his difficulty with a case. If the consultant had been successful in creating a group atmosphere which is generally supportive and nonjudgmental of feelings expressed, workers will often welcome a chance to acquire better understanding of their own involvements.

Under such favorable circumstances, one function of the consultant is to make a worker conscious of the attitude or feeling that underlies the trouble and to interpret it.

Before deciding to discuss a worker's personal involvement in a particular problem, the consultant must consider how far the conflict is from consciousness and how ego-alien. It is also worthwhile to consider how useful an emphasis on his own feelings would be in helping the worker solve that problem and how significant the conflict is to his general functioning. Even when there is clear evidence of a worker's personal involvement in a case, the consultant must realize that anxiety can sometimes be allayed more successfully by inference than by direct discussion.

As previously mentioned, training and experience in psychotherapy tend to bias a clinically oriented consultant toward focusing on the emotional reactions of individual members in a group, and while such emphasis is frequently indicated, the consultant must often exercise considerable clinical judgment in estimating the appropriate timing.

Knowledge of attitudes and ideas commonly shared by members of a particular profession affect a consultant's ability to allay guilt reactions which almost universally arise in certain situations. Individuals may be relieved of anxiety and may actually achieve considerable insight into sources of personal conflict through improved awareness of reactions common to the group as a whole. Whereas focus on the conflicts of any individual may be extremely damaging to morale of a group, workers can almost always accept insight into shared reactions. Consultation focused on problems common to a particular type of professional group may, therefore, have therapeutic effects upon individual members without directly attacking their personal resistances or defense systems.

A consultant's own interest in obtaining information from the group occasionally may cause him to raise a specific topic. A number of times in my own experience, ideas that came out in one group prompted me to direct the attention of subsequent groups to the same subject. This kind of activity eventually benefits workers by increasing a consultant's understanding of them and their problems, but for the most part, interests of the consultant should be subordinated to those expressed by the group.

CHAPTER IV

SHARED ATTITUDES OF WORKERS IN THREE PROFESSIONS

In the following section I have outlined some general characteristics shared by many individuals in the professions of public health nursing, nursery school education, and school teaching. These ideas were developed as I talked with workers in various professions over more than 10 years as leader of the in-service training program described in this book, as psychiatric consultant to guidance workers in a public school system, and as a faculty member both in the Center for Training in Community Psychiatry at Berkeley and in the experimental two-year program to train a psychiatrist as leader of in-service training for groups of school teachers which was also financed by the California State Department of Mental Hygiene before inception of the Center's more comprehensive program. In the course of this experience, I worked directly with many people in professions that are not psychologically oriented, and collected case material on others presented by guidance workers and psychiatrists. Statements included here are made on the basis of these personal observations and do not pretend to reflect intensive research on the psychological characteristics of various professional groups.

Although it is important to avoid stereotyping professional groups, it can be said that in each profession, the nature of work tends to attract individuals who, despite many dissimilarities, share certain personal qualities that are also accentuated through approval by their teachers and supervisors. The type of work itself also engenders specific attitudes and arouses anxieties common to members of the group, regardless of personal traits or neurotic conflicts of any one member. A profession leaves its stamp on workers, and conversely, workers leave their stamp on a profession. Although I believe that the generalizations made here are valid for a significant number of people in the various professional groups described, I sincerely hope that these observations will be elaborated and revised when more consultants from the psychological professions have reported their experiences with groups from the same professions.

The section on public health nurses is reproduced *in toto,* with minor editing, from a monograph (Parker, 1958) based on discussions with nurses between 1953 and 1957. In view of changed conditions in the country as a whole over the last 10 years, particularly those resulting from passage of the Medicare Act, certain observations may not be relevant any more, such as those about the collection of fees. I am letting them stand because I think the situation described is representative of a general tendency for nurses to have conflicts about duties requiring them to violate their ideal image of the nurse's role.

The section on nursery school teachers reproduces without change all but the first few paragraphs of a previously published article (Parker, 1962). The section on hidden attitudes in the educational system is the complete reproduction of a previously unpublished article addressed to community psychiatrists.

PUBLIC HEALTH NURSES

To select the bases, principles, and goals of in-service training for public health nurses, we need as clear a picture of the public health nurse and her job as can be drawn. To this end, I have tried to characterize her, using the emotional reactions, needs, self-image, and even the personality type most commonly revealed by nurses with whom I have worked.

Emotional Reactions

Emotional reactions aroused in most public health nurses on the job include: sensitivity in dealing with problems of dirt and body odors in patients, anxiety about intruding where they feel unwanted, guilt for their own prejudices and passive wishes, hostility toward patients who reject their services, and, frequently, hostility toward patients who exhibit what the nurse considers immoral or irresponsible attitudes. The last category includes people who are living in extramarital relationships, mothers of illegitimate children, indigent families who continue to have children while on public assistance, "neglectful" parents, venereal disease patients, and homosexuals. Since much of the work of a public health nurse necessitates frequent contact with such elements, they must be able to recognize and control their own emotional reactions if they are to function efficiently.

Self-image

To a public health nurse, the ideal member of her profession is a selfless giver whose chief motivation is a desire to teach, counsel, and give practical aid to people in all walks of life. She sees as her realm any area which affects the physical, emotional, or social health of people in her community.

A nurse's emotional reactions are closely related to her own personality structure and to her self-image in the role of public health nurse. Despite the widely differing personalities encountered in the nursing profession and the range of social and political philosophies represented, there is a striking uniformity in certain aspects of the picture nurses have of themselves. People take up public health nursing for a variety of conscious personal reasons and because of different unconscious motivations. However, certain personality needs are filled to some extent by a job which demands routine services to people of widely varying socio-economic backgrounds. If the nurse is to get satisfaction from her contacts with all these different people, she must see herself, and wants others to see her, as a certain kind of person. Whatever the unconscious need for such an image, the image is uniform in the consciousness of many public health nurses.

It is important for nurses to believe that they are establishing a quality of personal relationship satisfying to patients and to themselves. In order for the relationship to be satisfying to the nurse, however, she must be able to feel she can reach the professional goal set for herself in each case. If, after the establishment of rapport, a patient fails to heed the nurse's advice and suggestions, her goal recedes. She feels frustrated and has a tendency to lose the satisfaction previously derived from contact with the patient.

Training of public health nurses seems to accentuate the desire to "do something" for people, to teach procedures, and to induce the adoption of "correct" health practices. The average public health nurse enjoys interaction with people, for it fills a need in her own personality. However, to get real personal satisfaction from relationships with her patients, she must feel that such relationships are in harmony with her image of the nurse's role. She must sometimes be made aware that in maintaining a friendly human contact she is actually carrying out an important nursing function.

Many nurses say that one reason they prefer public health nursing to hospital nursing is that it enables them to develop long-term relationships and permits them to see the end results of their contacts with people. School nursing is particularly satisfying in this respect, because of the continued association with growing children and their parents over a period of years. On the other hand, nurses who have worked in a unified nursing service which provides various types of nursing opportunities, even though they do not prefer bedside nursing, say the visiting-nurse aspects of their job add variety and the enjoyment of a broadened participation in life of the community. "Chronics" and geriatric patients tend to create anxiety and a feeling of helplessness in many nurses. However, nurses often come to realize that they help such patients by maintaining a personal relationship that transcends the routine services they perform. A feeling of being "really needed," not only for physical care but as a welcome personality in the home, can give great satisfaction to a public health nurse.

A threat to the long-term "giving" quality of a relationship to patients creates conflict in a nurse about several types of routine nursing activity. A necessity to collect payment for her services constitutes such a threat to the self-image of many nurses.

In Berkeley, it has been a policy of the Visiting Nurse Association to allow nurses to reduce standard fees for home services in cases of need. From several group discussions, it became evident that decisions about setting fees are almost always made on a highly subjective basis and bear little relationship to financial realities. Many a nurse feels strongly that a financial transaction destroys something in the relationship between nurse and patient that is valuable to both. She fears that her patients will feel the same disappointment in her that she herself feels for her inability to be a "selfless giver," serving without recompense.

The nurse's feeling of guilt about taking payment for service is particularly acute if the patient is in pain or is suffering from an incurable disease. In such cases, the nurse is apt to undercharge or not charge at all, regardless of the patient's financial status. To a nurse, the fee is a punitive measure, and if she can dissociate herself from it in the eyes of a patient, she feels less guilty. On the other hand, if a patient is "demanding" or "ungrateful," the nurse may charge a full fee with the same disregard of financial criteria as she displays in cases of need.

Although conflicts about charges for medical services are common among both members of the public and members of the medical profession, for nurses this problem seems related to the need for a benign image of their role. Political and philosophical attitudes of individual nurses toward private practice and free medical care also influence the ease with which the financial aspect of the nurse's job can be handled. Nurses who have had considerable experience in private duty have the least difficulty in collecting a fee, while those who have most fully subscribed to public health philosophy feel the most guilt. Some nurses avoid the problem by merely asking the patient if he or she wishes to be billed by the health department. Some discuss fees with the patient before a relationship has been established so that feelings about money will not intrude upon the situation once they are functioning as nurses. Those who have the fewest personal conflicts in this area have the least trouble making a fee acceptable to the patient.

Similar conflict complicates the determination of whether a child should be recommended for free school lunch, a decision often left to the nurse. In this situation she is caught between a feeling of guilt toward the taxpayer, usually instilled in her by superiors, and her own strong feeling that a child should never go hungry, no matter what the financial circumstances of the family.

Here again, value judgments about "attitude" and the degree of sympathy for a particular family influence her decision far more than financial criteria. If the nurse feels that a family will spend what they save on a child's lunch to give him other advantages, she is apt to be more lenient than if the family is "selfish" or "demanding." All nurses with whom I have talked, however, feel that a child should not suffer for parental bad management and that, if there is any question of deprivation, lunch should certainly be furnished by the school. Any attempt by the school or health administration to cast a nurse in the role of "one who withholds nourishment" will cause anxiety and resentment. The nurse's consciousness of a protective relationship to children is a primary satisfaction of school work.

An even stronger element in motivation toward public health nursing than toward other branches of nursing seems to be the nurse's need for recognition as an independent, responsible, professional person, regarded as an equal by members of other professions. Whenever anything, either from inside the nurse herself or from attitudes in the environment, threatens her feeling of personal status, anxious conflict is generated.

The public health nurse feels that in hospital work or private duty she is relegated to the position of "flunky to the doctor and rich neurotics." Although she gets some satisfaction from those aspects of Visiting Nurse Association work in which she is relieving pain and giving physical comfort, she often feels that her status increases in direct proportion to the distance her work is removed from the physical care of patients. I have found this to be a common feeling throughout all teaching professions. Nursery school teachers, for example, feel that the public accords them less status than it does grade school teachers almost entirely because of the actual physical care required by small children. This feeling seems to be at least one of the major reasons why nurses prefer to emphasize the teaching and counseling aspects of public health nursing.

The same feeling influences a nurse's attitude toward wearing a uniform. In large metropolitan areas, where most public health nursing is performed among the lowest socioeconomic classes, the uniform is regarded as a protection and a symbol of high status; but in a community like Berkeley, the nurse generally considers it "the label of an enema giver." Nurses value the privilege of wearing civilian clothes and entering patients' homes as "visitors." Dressed as visitors, they feel they encounter one less barrier to establishment of the kind of nurse-patient relationship which offers them the most satisfaction. This is especially true in the higher socioeconomic districts, where many nurses feel their status to be relatively insecure.

When a nurse is looked up to by her patients, she invariably feels more confident in executing her nursing functions. A striking example of this is the relative ease with which such delicate problems as body odor and dirt can be discussed with offenders from the lower-class districts. The nurse's rationalization is that patients from these areas are less sensitive about having the subject mentioned. When the dirty patient is a college professor's child, "speaking to" the parents becomes a dreaded and difficult chore requiring extreme delicacy, despite the obvious fact that if a "Bohemian" in rebellion against middle-class standards of cleanliness were sensitive to criticism about it, he would not have allowed it to occur.

The importance of a nurse's position in the school and her view of her status affects her functioning as a school nurse. She takes pride in being a member of the school faculty and feels hurt and resentful if she thinks other members of the faculty regard her as a routine dispenser of first aid. In fact, the degree to which she feels respected by her colleagues in the school determines to a great extent her satisfaction with the job.

Often there is a sharp conflict between health department and school administration personnel regarding the proper duties of a nurse in the schools, although the attitudes of school personnel vary considerably. However, if a nurse establishes friendly relations with the faculty in her school and becomes trusted personally, she is frequently able to impress her superiors with her usefulness in a kind of role for which she considers herself best qualified.

School personnel are not always accustomed to viewing neurotic behavior in children as a health problem falling within the jurisdiction of the nurse. Before teachers and parents will accept the nurse as a counselor, she must repeatedly demonstrate her understanding and helpfulness. Nurses, on the other hand, often do not realize that the attitudes of school personnel are rooted in traditional concepts of nursing which may not have kept pace with recent trends in the training of public health nurses. It does not occur to them that regular school personnel may think of them as outsiders because they only work part time in the school, and they feel personally snubbed by what is considered a devaluation of their function. When this happens, the morale and efficiency of the nurse decreases.

To summarize, any threat to a nurse's status or to the quality of her relationship with patients makes for a feeling of insecurity in carrying out her role. Her satisfaction in the job depends on preserving a feeling that she is fulfilling her ideal of what a public health nurse should be and do, and that the public values her in that role.

Personality Type

The public health nurse who chooses to work in a unified nursing service has interests and seeks job satisfactions more like those of the social worker than like those of the hospital nurse. Higher pay and better hours seem to rate second to the fulfillment of personal needs for active interrelationship with varied groups of people throughout the community. A nearby city offers the opportunity to do school nursing alone, with its shorter hours and long vacations. These jobs are a great temptation to many nurses, particularly those with families of their own. But surprisingly, during the 10 years of my association with the health department, relatively few nurses left the unified service for what they all considered an easier job. It would seem that nurses who want only school nursing, and those who choose a Visiting Nurse Association program confined exclusively to physical care of patients in their homes, are of somewhat different personality types from the nurses who choose and stay with a unified service. The stimulation of a job combining bedside nursing, school nursing, and various other types of activity attracts a person with broad interests and a community-oriented outlook.

NURSERY SCHOOL TEACHERS

This section discusses ideas and feelings I frequently encountered in diverse groups of nursery school teachers during weekly interviews over a 10-year period. An attempt will be made to clarify the sources and effects of such ideas and to indicate ways in which a consultant can prevent them from interfering with the effective functioning of the teachers.

In the vast majority of topics that I heard raised by nursery school teachers, 10 ideas appeared prominently and seemed to be generally shared.

1. It is unprofessional for a teacher to become angry with a child or his parent(s).
2. If you understand a problem, you should be able to solve it.
3. "Permissiveness" is good, "authoritarianism" is bad (or vice versa).
4. A really good teacher never dislikes a child.
5. A teacher should be able to help all children who show an obvious need.
6. A prime goal of nursery school is to help all children become "integrated with the group."
7. It is an important part of the teacher's job to help parents develop "healthy relationships" with their children. To do so, the teacher's role is one of counseling mothers and understanding their personal problems.
8. Disturbed parents or family relationships always produce disturbed children.
9. A disturbed child will always be found to have a disturbed family.
10. If a teacher does feel anger, dislike, or any other "undesirable" feeling, she must control any recognizable expression of it.

Some of these ideas are entirely erroneous, and some are true under certain conditions but not under others. Some of these ideas set up stereotypes which make it difficult for teachers to use their trained perception of *observable behavior* in order to make a correct evaluation of individual situations. These ideas are involved in many of the conflicts that impede the ability of teachers to deal adequately with the problems of children and parents in their schools.

I found that in a large number of situations with which nursery school teachers were having difficulty, there was evidence of guilt among the teachers for having feelings that, although perfectly normal and understandable, they felt they should not be having. Frequently this guilt made them feel they should hide or counteract these feelings. Whenever they did so, they became uneasy and lost objectivity toward the problem. In most cases, they had all the knowledge necessary to handle the problem successfully but were unable to use it effectively because of their guilt.

I shall try to indicate some of the ways in which these ideas create difficulties and some of the ways in which these difficulties may be prevented.

First of all, a feeling that anger on the job is unacceptable has seemed to me nearly universal among nursery school teachers. Often they cannot admit even to themselves that they feel angry with, or dislike any child. No matter how much provocation they have had, if they become angry, they feel guilty. They frequently try to hide the anger by being especially patient and understanding with the child.

It is an empirical fact, however, that when a person tries to hide an attitude or feeling, the impact of the hidden attitude upon the other person is apt to be even greater than it would have been if the attitude had been openly expressed. The person who is trying to hide the attitude is hampered in her capacity to resolve the problem, and the reaction of one exposed to the hidden attitude is either confusion or mistrust. Such distortions in the interaction between teacher and child can be prevented in various ways if the source of the guilty emotion is clarified and the guilt is reduced.

The commonest causes for anger with or dislike of a child fall into two categories: (1) Realistic causes, which cannot be avoided, and should be recognized. (2) Displaced causes, which can be avoided if real sources of the feeling are recognized.

Realistic Reasons for Anger

1. The child behaves in a way that creates immediate danger to himself or others. No matter how "understanding" one may be, such behavior is frightening to everyone and evokes instantaneous, spontaneous anger. I do not believe this can be avoided. Also, it is actually useful for the child to recognize that people react in that way when he endangers himself or others.

2. The child makes a painful personal attack such as kicking a person hard in the shins. Everyone becomes angry under these circumstances, and it is unrealistic not to show it.

3. A child is purposely naughty in a way that he could very well control and disrupts group activity. If the teacher tries to act as though she is not angry, she will not help the child to learn acceptable ways of behaving. She can control the *way* in which she shows her feelings, but if she tries to cover them up, her own ability to handle the situation may be damaged. The child will not be fooled, and his ability to come to grips with realistic demands may be impaired.

The second category of situations, in which teachers get angry at children may be more preventable. This includes cases in which anger has its origins elsewhere and is displaced onto the child.

Causes for Displaced Anger

1. Feelings about the parents. If a teacher does not like the child's father or mother for any number of conscious or unconscious reasons, the feeling may rub off on the child.

2. Frustration with the child's problem. If the needs of the child make a teacher feel helpless, she may dislike him.

3. Competitive or hostile feelings toward other teachers. If, for instance, there is some disagreement between two teachers and a particular child is attached to one of them, the other may not like him.

4. Reaction to not being loved by a child. This is exceedingly common. Everyone who chooses to work with little children tends to respond to a child who responds to her, and vice versa. All adults find certain children more appealing than others, although the type of child found appealing varies greatly among individuals. If a child has the kind of personality that makes him hostile, cold, or indifferent to adults, many teachers will not care for him, although they will all feel very guilty about it. They believe that an understanding of his problem should make them immune from reacting to his hostility.

In all of these cases, when a teacher recognizes what her feelings really are and why they occur, she often has a marked change of feeling toward the child; she is able to see *him* clearly, without impairment of her objectivity. When it is not possible for her to like a particular child, she should be helped to overcome her guilt. It is seldom possible for every teacher to like every child in a school. There is often one teacher in a group who likes a particular child better than another teacher does, and if there is a problem, there is no reason why the one who likes him should not be allowed to assume major responsibility in his case. No matter what the administrative setup in any school, I have never encountered a situation in which such a change could not be arranged easily when the advisability of making a change was accepted without guilt or recrimination. I have seen a number of cases in which an intense need to "work through" the negative feelings for which a teacher felt guilty resulted in a prolonged struggle in which neither the child, the teacher, nor the rest of the group profited.

Teachers are commonly made angry by certain kinds of parents.

Parents Who Anger Teachers

1. Parents who "mistreat" their children. Individual teachers vary in their opinion as to what constitutes mistreatment, but if a teacher feels a parent is being cruel, she invariably has strong feelings about it (as do most people).

2. Mothers who put their relationships to husbands and boyfriends ahead of their responsibility to the child. Almost all teachers with whom I consulted seemed to feel some resentment toward a mother who is relatively neglectful of the needs of her child when they conflict with her pursuit of a husband.

3. Parents whose value system differs markedly from that of the teachers. Rigid, Bohemian, dirty, careless, irreligious people, for instance, will have different effects upon different teachers depending upon whether the teachers themselves value religion, conformity, etc., and what their own standards of cleanliness are.

4. Parents who, for any reason, seem to "look down" on the teachers, or do not recognize their professional training. Skilled nursery school teachers are frequently very defensive against any implication that they are "glorified baby-sitters."

5. Parents who, for any reason, criticize the school. The need for good public relations has been a very real problem, particularly in agencies whose support comes from public funds which have to be renewed periodically.

Anyone who is critical becomes a threat to the existence of the school, even if the teachers recognize the hostilities as a neurotic problem in the parent.

Whenever anger arises for any of these reasons, the teacher is apt to create a reaction formation against it and to become unusually understanding and patient. She feels she has to do this because to admit anger is unacceptable. Unfortunately, the real feeling usually creeps through somehow and damages her effectiveness.

Consultants can help teachers to admit anger by emphasizing that it is normal under certain circumstances and that some displacement exists in all professional workers. Teachers can be encouraged to discharge their anger either to supervisors, among themselves, or in a consultation group.

Support and reassurance from administrative levels is important in keeping down the anger that arises from fear for their jobs. Understanding the needs of parents as well as children may cut down on resentments that arise from the "child-centered" attitudes that are *normal* among people who choose to work with children.

Unavoidable anger simply has to be discharged, although not necessarily toward the "cruel" parent (who sometimes is not nearly as cruel by her own standards as she is by the standards of the teachers). In any case, a teacher must get rid of the anger, not pretend she doesn't have it. This is necessary if she is to avoid displacing it onto the child.

Another source of guilt is the feeling that teachers should be able to help all children according to their needs and that understanding a problem inevitably leads to its solution. Often after teachers have had some experience with consultation, a myth will begin to arise that "talking a problem over" will always make it disappear. Sometimes this does happen, through relief of the tension-creating anxiety of the teacher group, but sometimes teachers develop an almost magical expectation that it will and are filled with guilt and disappointment if it does not.

Often the needs of an individual child conflict with the needs of the group as a whole, and a teacher is thrown into conflict over the nature of her responsibility. Some may have to choose between damaging the morale of the group or taking a course that is less than ideal from the standpoint of an individual child.

There are times when an individual child has such overwhelming emotional needs that they cannot possibly be met fully, no matter how hard the teacher tries. In such cases, the teacher feels helpless, and a vicious cycle may occur. The feeling of helplessness may make her angry at the child who provoked it, but the anger makes her guilty, and the need to counteract that anger makes her feel still more helpless. Anger is a normal reaction to helplessness. The need to deny the feeling leads to displacements and reaction formations that interfere with a clear view of what is happening in an interaction, thus impeding realistic solution of the problem.

In situations of this kind, it is important to help the teacher realize that some children just cannot be helped as much as she would like to help them. Recognition of this fact reduces the teacher's own feeling of helplessness and frustration and cuts down on the personal sense of threat which makes her angry with the child. When she begins to feel irrational anger or dislike of a child whose intense needs are obvious, she should be encouraged to recognize her own need to be infallible. She can best be helped to face it if she realizes that, to one degree or another, it is shared by everyone in her line of work.

I believe that certain problems arise directly from confusion in applying knowledge about psychodynamics and emotional development. Psychoanalytic principles have become increasingly well-known in the last 20 years, and their misapplication to practical situations has done a lot of damage to both parents and teachers.

One particularly destructive misconception is the idea that it is good to allow a child completely free expression of aggression and hostility whenever he feels angry.[1] "Permissiveness" in regard to feelings is, of course, not synonymous with a lack of limits on a child's behavior, but nursery school teachers often seem to think they will be criticized or thought "old-fashioned" if they put any restraints upon the way in which a child expresses rage and frustration. The big problem that arises under these circumstances is again apt to be development of the "hidden attitude." It results in what I like to call "rule by indirection."

Teachers, as well as parents and many other people today, think they *ought* to feel permissive, but in reality they do not. They really feel they should have some control over a child's choices, but feel guilty about it. Therefore, they frequently offer the child a choice that turns out to be no choice at all. They want to make a child self-reliant by permitting him to choose between various alternatives, but if the child chooses something they cannot accept as wise, they try to make him change his mind without letting him know they are trying to manipulate him. They want him to think the choice is his own. This makes for lots of confusion in the child's mind.

However, hidden authoritarianism is very prevalent in our culture today, creating emotional disturbances that range from mild to exceedingly serious. A consultant can

---

[1] Today many people within and without the educational system at all levels espouse a philosophy of freedom to a degree that can be extremely destructive to young people, raising rather than lowering their anxieties and tensions.

help teachers to recognize their own tendencies to indulge in this very common practice and help them to avoid it. A teacher must determine the degree of permissiveness with which she feels comfortable and act accordingly. Even if some teachers are too strict and others too lenient, they will be successful on the whole with most of the children in their charge if they act according to the way they feel and do not try to hide an opposing attitude.

Psychiatric knowledge has also had a tendency to create conflict over the concept of need for "integration with the group." Recognition that a withdrawn child may have emotional problems that need attention tends to make teachers feel that any child who prefers to play alone is maladjusted. An individual child may be quite normal and still prefer at times to be outside the group. Whether or not this tendency is an indication of maladjustment should be evaluated on the basis of the child's *total* observable behavior and attitudes.

However, acceptance by teachers of a stereotype regarding the need to be "adjusted to the group" may impair their ability to make such an evaluation according to their experience and knowledge of behavioral signs. When a consultant senses that a stereotype has developed, he can help reorient the teachers to focusing on total observable behavior.

Emphasis during a nursery school teacher's training on the importance of her role as a parent-counselor has opened up another source of guilt for the teacher. I have seen many cases in which a teacher's desire to help a mother to improve her relationship to her child has caused the teacher to become more deeply embroiled in the personal affairs of the mother than either she or the mother feels comfortable about.

Anxiety about the degree of involvement may lead to guilt and insecurity in handling the problem. The teacher may become confused and the mother angry. If the mother accuses the teacher of being intrusive, the teacher's own guilt may be expressed in retaliatory punitiveness toward the mother.

Here again, it is important to help teachers set limits on a counseling relationship at the point where they feel comfortable and secure. If a mother needs more than the teacher feels she can offer, the mother can be directed toward the kind of facility available for further pursuit of the problem with someone specifically trained in the techniques of psychotherapy.

Counseling by nursery school teachers is most useful to mothers if it is directed toward increasing the mother's understanding of the child's behavior and the feelings reflected by that behavior. The teacher can make use of her trained observations of the kind of behavior observable at school and help the mother to be more tolerant and understanding of normal developmental stages. The mother's anxiety will thereby be reduced without the application of any specific therapy for her internal conflicts.

Even though a teacher may herself have a clear understanding of the reasons for emotional tensions in a child, and may feel them to be connected with a mother's own neurotic problems, the teacher is not trained in the techniques for making interpretations to a mother about disturbed family relationships. When she tries to do so, she often gets into a situation which arouses anxiety in herself and anger in the mother. Her effectiveness in helping the mother is reduced. A consultant can help teachers determine the best level for their interventions.

Another misconception promoted by training is the assumption that a child is disturbed just because his family is upset, or that a family must necessarily be pathological because a child has symptoms of emotional unrest. These conditions often go together, but not *always*. Sometimes a child from a highly disturbed background remains relatively healthy for a number of reasons that are not always apparent. Sometimes, too, a child's aggressive behavior results from inner conflicts that persist despite a relatively benign current family situation. A teacher may misperceive the child if she has a tendency to accept the stereotype. A consultant can encourage her to avoid this pitfall by focusing on the child's observable behavior.

A relatively small, but also significant, number of problems presented by nursery school teachers have their origins in the personal conflicts of the individual teachers. Whatever the variation may be in the individual sources or expressions of such conflicts, they seem to fall into four general categories.

1. *Projection of the teacher's childhood hurts onto a child.* A teacher reacts to the child's difficulty as though it were identical with something she herself suffered as a child. She often cannot see that the child's reaction has a different explanation, because she is overidentified with one aspect of his problem. For instance, a minority-group teacher may interpret a fight between two children as evidence of racial prejudice, when actually it may have quite a different explanation.

2. *Projection of the teacher's relationships with authority onto other relationships.* If a teacher has difficulty with a supervisor or consultant, she may need to counteract her own feelings of helplessness by acting toward one of the mothers as she feels the supervisor is acting toward her. On the other hand, she may act toward the mother as she wishes the supervisor would act toward her, even though the actual basis of interaction may be quite different.

3. *Projection of problems the teacher has with her own children onto other mothers.* The teacher sees another mother's difficulty with her child as similar to one that the teacher has with her own child. She cannot

perceive the differences, again because of identification with one aspect of the mother-child relationship.

4. Rationalization or reaction formation to personal feelings of repugnance to dirt, racial prejudice, professional rivalry, or any other "unacceptable feeling."

A consultant does not need to go into the individual's personal reasons for such feelings. He may be most helpful by demonstrating the universality of personal conflicts in even "well-adjusted" people and by exploding the misconceptions that exist regarding a need for perfection in teachers.

One of the misuses of psychodynamic knowledge that is becoming increasingly widespread among people who deal with other people professionally is propagation of the concept that all such professional people are supposed to be perfectly well-adjusted and without evidence of any personality problems. Nothing could be farther from the truth! The myth of the "perfectly analyzed analyst" is no sillier than the myth of the "perfectly loving and understanding" nursery school teacher.

A consultant can point out that certain built-in attitudes and personality characteristics are frequent in all people who choose to work professionally with children, just as the same is true for people who choose other kinds of professions. Such attitudes and feelings are always reflected to some degree in their interactions with others on the job. Training can teach that certain ways of expressing feelings are more useful than others. Knowledge and experience help to overcome certain feelings that may have antedated entrance into any field, and it is hoped that most professional workers continue to change their attitudes throughout their careers. Some feelings, even unacceptable ones, however, will always be with us. The important thing is to be aware of them and create realistic interpersonal relationships. This is most important for people who are working with children and hoping to help them build sound emotional attitudes.

PUBLIC SCHOOL TEACHERS

Stereotypes of school teachers are apt to be exceedingly prevalent in the population. Along with doctors and ministers, teachers fall into a category of professional workers upon whom many people project parental transference and who arouse considerable ambivalence as representatives of childhood authority figures. In actuality, extremely diverse personality types are found in the teaching profession as a whole. Some people who are clinically trained in psychological principles tend at times to forget that many individuals without such specific training have considerable intuitive awareness of human reactions and knowledge about what underlies the behavior of those with whom they interact in their own kind of work. A great number of school teachers are drawn into this kind of work by a real interest in and understanding of children. Many, both experienced and inexperienced, are dedicated people who have the best interests of their pupils *and the pupils' families* deeply at heart and serve those interests often at considerable self-sacrifice without much inner conflict. There are others, of course, who are drawn into teaching for many other reasons and about whom the opposite of the above could be said. Since generalizations about the group as a whole are exceedingly dangerous, I will confine my comments to a very few attitudes which, in my experience, may be found in many school teachers and which may serve as a useful focus for the consultant if and when he encounters them.

Those teachers who are relatively unsophisticated about psychological concepts, which includes the majority, view disturbed behavior in children primarily as a discipline problem rather than as an illness; intellectually they may accept other views but unconsciously they may resist them for a variety of reasons. Even teachers who have been consciously convinced of a need to understand the motivations of their pupils often react punitively to behavior, no matter what its origin, which distracts others in the classroom or interferes with the ability of class members (including the disturbed child himself) to learn subject matter prescribed by the curriculum. Along with school administrators and supervisors, a teacher sees her primary job as teaching specific material, which is often required at a state level. Her prestige as an educator depends to some extent on how well her pupils pass standardized tests, and she tends to feel successful only with children who can learn well and can be taught to exert self-control in classroom and playground behavior. She reacts with anxiety or hostility to any concept that threatens her self-image as a good teacher. She is also threatened by anything that she feels may bring disapproval by any authority figure.

Teachers are made anxious by any knowledge that brings their attitudes into conflict with established policies in the educational system. In particular, those who attended progressive colleges as undergraduates and were frustrated by more authoritarian demands at teacher-training institutions may be threatened with reactivation of rebellion when a consultant supports ideas which they share but are unable to put into practice. More psychologically sophisticated teachers are often thrown into conflict between a wish to be more permissive and a personal or externally imposed need to act in an authoritarian way. This conflict has already been mentioned in connection with shared attitudes of nursery school teachers, and some of its results will be further elaborated in the next chapter.

Because the ability to keep a "quiet classroom" has so traditionally been regarded as the hallmark of a good teacher, some individuals may be disturbed to learn that a quiet classroom does not invariably promote the best interests of all children; in fact, under some circumstances learning is facilitated by a more relaxed atmosphere. Nowadays such ideas are being widely disseminated by educators who have become attuned to the special needs of "culturally deprived" children, but by and large they are not accepted as applying to the ordinary public school. "Keeping order" has become a goal in itself. Its value is taken for granted by most school administrators, who demand it of teachers, regardless of the circumstances, and criticize those who for any reason fail to attain the goal. On the other hand, an increasing number of administrators and teachers espouse a pseudotherapeutic philosophy concerning the value of "free expression of feelings" which approaches encouragement of anarchy in the classroom and may cause great disturbance to the security of an individual classroom teacher. Anxiety results from any conflict between a teacher's own need for approval and her concept of children's emotional needs.

Many teachers have reactions similar to those described for public health nurses concerning people who offend middle-class mores or who do not appreciate the value of a middle-class-oriented educational system. Even individual educators who themselves lead unconventional lives often subscribe to the idea that a public school teacher's duty is to instill conservative norms and concepts of morality into their pupils. Emphasis on didactic methods of teaching during their own professional training has encouraged many teachers to attack "deviant" behavior by preaching or moralizing, either openly or in subtle ways, and anxiety will be aroused by the idea that such methods usually do not change the children's attitudes. Others, particularly those who have taken an interest in movements attempting to benefit the underprivileged, tend to feel that any child from a middle-class suburban environment must necessarily be inhibited and out of contact with his parents; such teachers are threatened by the idea that encouragement to abandon conventional modes of dress and behavior will not always "loosen up" the child to his benefit.

Anxiety or hostility will regularly be aroused by anything a teacher interprets as casting aspersion on her ability to understand children. Most educators believe that an intuitive knowledge of child psychology requires nothing more than "common sense," and feel that they possess it, regardless of the reactions of their pupils.

A consultant may pick up considerable evidence that many conscious and unconscious conflicts arise in teachers because of their reactions to parents, particularly if they have children of their own. As in the case of nursery school teachers, attitudes toward a child's parents may be displaced onto the child, or a teacher may overidentify with the child's parent; but more often the teacher overidentifies with the child and needs to undo her own childhood hurts by simultaneously taking on the role of "good mother" in competition with the child's own mother. A regressive pull is exerted upon teachers by the classroom atmosphere, and, particularly in cases where the teacher is herself only a few years removed from experience as a school child, conflicts with parental figures can be unconsciously reawakened.

HIDDEN ATTITUDES IN THE EDUCATIONAL SYSTEM

Many consultants and counselors are struggling to make those in close contact with the children more aware of important factors in child development so that a healthy emotional climate can be created for the children. It is well recognized that the unconscious attitudes of professional personnel are crucial to success or failure in the application of any educational or child-rearing theory. Attitudes which are deeply unconscious or rooted in character structure are, of course, inaccessible to alteration through the limited kinds of discussion available in programs of consultation or in-service training. I have demonstrated in previous chapters, however, that workers have certain conscious or preconscious attitudes which they try to conceal either because such attitudes are ego-alien or alien to their professional image. Such attitudes can be significantly influenced if the consultant is aware of their prevalence and potential interference with the professional task.

I have touched on some of the attitudes frequently shared by members of such helping professions as public health nursing and nursery school teaching, pointing out among other things some of the problems created when an attitude of "masked authoritarianism" is displayed by professional workers or parents. Here I shall discuss masked authoritarianism further in the more general context of attitudes which teachers (and other professional workers) feel as ego-alien and which they attempt to hide in various ways from their pupils (or clients). Since undistorted communication between a pupil and his teacher is essential if the pupil is to learn, hidden attitudes on the part of those who are attempting to teach are often grossly damaging to their task. Over many years of association with different sorts of teaching groups, I have found that such hidden attitudes pervade the educational system at all levels and that they cause many problems which bother workers. They are a major source of distortion in professional and personal relationships and are particularly destructive in the relationships between adults and children. Consultants always should be on the lookout for them and point out their damaging effects to those who display them.

A child's whole concept of reality depends upon his ability to believe the evidence imparted by his own senses and to trust that his parents and teachers are reliable sources of information and authority. In order to feel secure with adults, a child must know that he meets with their approval. If he does not, he must know exactly why not and how he must change his behavior in order to do so. He must be able to perceive the demands that are made upon him clearly and to know the truth about his relationships with the people upon whom he depends as guides and models. Overt expressions by parents and teachers which belie their true feelings not only confuse children but also may undermine their trust and produce open anxiety or distorted behavior.

Most people who deal with children wish to be honest and help the children acquire a realistic view of the world. However, at times most people also react to children with attitudes or feelings that are ego-alien or that they believe to be condemned by others such as their own professional preceptors. Such attitudes or feelings may be unconscious or conscious, or they may be based on ideas that are often simply taken for granted without question in middle-class culture. When such reactions occur, adults frequently try to hide them from the children by presenting rationalizations or by practicing various forms of deception which lie along a curve from the well-meaning evasions that almost everyone practices at one time or another "in the child's best interest," to the grossest lies and denials of reality. The tendency to carry out the milder forms of conscious, well-intentioned deception is so prevalent in the United States that it might be said to constitute a norm in adult-child interactions. Evidence that it is also prevalent in the kibbutzim of Israel can be noted in Spiro's book on the educational system there (Spiro, 1958) and could doubtless be found almost everywhere in the world. However, whenever dishonesty or conspicuous indirectness enters into the relationship of a child with a person meaningful to him, it may damage the child's ability to cope realistically with his environment and his emotional responses to it.

At this time in history, despite efforts to be aware of lower-class culture, school personnel in our country are predominantly oriented toward a middle-class value system and believe sincerely that any child who is to be successful in our society must adopt middle-class values, which include taboos on overt expresssions of aggression and upon any reference to the genital or excretory apparatus or functions of the body and which stress cleanliness and learning for their own sake. Whenever for any reason children do not seem motivated to adopt these standards, many teachers are threatened in the exercise of their role as guides and models, and anxiety is evoked.

Although it is well known that anxiety may take the form of repugnance, prejudice, or anger toward the individual who evokes it, such attitudes expressed openly toward a child are ego-alien to a majority of the professional people who work with children. Teachers think that negative feelings toward children must be hidden. When such hiding takes place consciously or preconsciously, subtle hypocrisies, insincerities, and lacks of clarity result, which have an effect both on the child and the adult which may be as destructive to their relationship as the expression of more deeply unconscious hostility. A few examples from cases that I have encountered in consultation with guidance personnel and nursery or elementary school teachers may clarify this point.

1. In a burst of temper, a rebellious nursery school child threw finger paint on his teacher's clean blouse. She told him she was not angry but disappointed to see that he was "that kind of a boy." The child sensed suppressed anger (which he obviously expected in any case) in her

voice, but became confused in distinguishing her reaction to this specific act from her feeling about him as a total individual. He began to feel that she considered him a "bad boy" in general, and other aspects of their relationship deteriorated.

2. A ten-year-old boy had been referred to a guidance worker because of persistent body odor and filth. The worker called him in on the pretext that he had been referred because of difficulties with his school work and offered him her friendship without ever mentioning the problem of cleanliness. Through long experience, the child had learned to sense aversion and evasiveness. Having no reason to believe this worker was different from anyone else, he lost confidence in a relationship to the person who, through frank acceptance of his problem, might have gained his cooperation in having to discover the source of his need to present himself so unattractively.

3. A young junior high school teacher had encouraged his class to write a composition about "anything you want." A boy wrote of violent hatred toward the school and everyone in it, describing in graphic terms what he would like to do to some of the female teachers. Several times in the next few days he asked the teacher whether the compositions had yet been read, but the teacher put him off. Later in the week, the boy was referred to the guidance department on another pretext. Nobody in the school ever mentioned the composition to him. The guidance contact failed, and a hitherto good relationship between the boy and his own teacher was damaged by evasive handling of the obvious plea for an open discussion of his feelings.

4. A six-year-old boy fell on the playground and skidded on his front along the asphalt, causing a slight but profusely bleeding laceration of his penis. The female teacher called the janitor to determine the extent of the injury and

to report the accident to the male principal. The principal, in calling for the mother, refused to discuss the nature of the accident over the phone, leaving her to arrive at school under the impression that her child had been critically injured. The whole incident, handled with such anxiety and evasion by all concerned, had considerable anxious impact on the child himself, although he had previously been relaxed and free in his attitudes toward his body.

In all these examples, the personnel involved were *consciously* aware of negative or prudish reactions but felt it necessary to avoid direct expression of the problem to a child or his parents to protect their "feelings" or because admission of their own anger, disgust, or prudishness was unacceptable to them. Consciously hidden attitudes are not dispelled; they are simply expressed in devious ways, and their impact on both child and adult is apt to be greater than if the attitude had been openly acknowledged. The child reacts with confusion, anger, or mistrust. The adult who tries to hide his true feelings may either displace them or react with various expressions of guilt and anxiety that damage his effectiveness in resolving the child's problem. I have shown some of the effects of such a situation in a nursery school.

Overt expressions which run counter to underlying feelings result from less conscious mechanisms in the adult which range all the way from massive unconscious denial through preconscious reluctance to face unpleasant truth. An individual's awareness of the discrepancy between what he expresses and what he feels may vary from time to time. The impact of such expressions of discrepancy may vary with the degree to which a tendency to act insincerely pervades the *total* behavior of an adult toward a child. Misrepresentations of true attitudes, conscious, unconscious, or both, may occur only occasionally, or they may be consistently employed to an extent that destroys all possibility for honest communication. They may be employed only for a very specific purpose, with conscious intent to manipulate a particular aspect of the child's thinking, as illustrated by the following quotations from Spiro (1958):

> Nurses do not view "chores" as "work," reserving this label for activities of an entirely different nature. These . . . consist of various types of art work. . . . This is a deliberate socialization device. . . . The kibbutz attempts to impress its workers' ideology on [the children] at as early an age as possible by arbitrarily referring to certain play activities as work [p. 210].
>
> The system of passing and failing [in school work] . . . violates the kibbutz ideals of equality and equal opportunity. . . . Recently, however, examinations in the guise of 'questionnaires' have been introduced [p. 260].

Occasional obscurity in the meaning of a communication from a significant adult may have a strong impact upon a child largely because it is unusual. On the other hand, consistent small misrepresentations may take place within the framework of such an overwhelmingly positive relationship that the traumatic effects are few and subtle if they occur at all. The damaging effect of hidden attitudes, at whatever level of consciousness or pervasiveness, depends on the way in which all elements combine in the overall interaction between adult and child and on the importance which a relationship to that particular adult holds for the child. Occasional benign distortions in communication may not be taken too seriously. On the other hand, a child's distorted interpretation of anxieties which he senses in adults may add specific reinforcement to other sources of confusion or feelings of personal insecurity and tend to further the formation of unfavorable behavioral and emotional responses.

Teachers are very important people in the lives of many children not only because they are the purveyors of society's attitudes in general but also because they may be significant parent surrogates, particularly to children where family relationships are tenuous or disturbed. Teachers' attitudes often have a strong impact on children, and distortions in communication with a teacher may be almost as traumatic as those with a parent.

A large number of teachers to one degree or another profess "permissiveness" but actually employ indirect and covert means of manipulating a child's behavior. Such "masked authoritarianism" has become extremely prevalent in our society, particularly among educated, liberal people who, although they were reared in a more authoritarian family structure, adhere widely to ideals of democratic interaction and reject the idea of tyrannical disciplinary methods. As noted earlier, it is also prevalent in Israel, where the value system of kibbutz society breaks markedly with that of the cultures where most first-generation immigrants were brought up. This attitude results in a sort of pseudo democracy which can cause great conflict in children because of the discrepancy between the conscious and unconscious value systems of adults. Education has imbued the adults with a strong desire to be democratic in child-rearing, but there exists an equally strong unconscious or preconscious need to assume firm direction of the child's behavior. They must therefore assume control under the guise of offering freedom. Directiveness which must be denied may express a genuine conviction that "mother knows best," based on a positive identification with the parent's own authoritarian parents combined with guilt for having "undemocratic" ideas. On the other hand, it may reflect deeply unconscious hostility toward the child or what he stands for in the adult's previous experience. In any case, control which must be presented as its opposite almost always has a hostile impact on the child (or adult) subjected to it.

In another publication (Parker, 1965) I have described in detail the role played by a predominantly good and loving father's masked authoritarianism in contributing to the development of his son's obsessional character neurosis. The following examples have been displayed by teachers at various levels of the educational system. In all cases, the educators had good intentions and were quite unaware of their attempts at coercion.

1. In a nursery school short of staff because of illness among the teachers, all but one or two children agreed that they wanted to hear a story during their "free play" period. The teacher took considerable time trying to persuade the minority that hearing a story would be "more fun" than playing in another part of the room, but when they became somewhat violent in their refusal, the teacher decided they were "tired" and had better rest on their cots. The children decided to "choose" the story.

2. A group of sixth graders in a public school were offered an "opportunity" to make "voluntary" contributions to a good cause. After it was found that a significant number had not contributed, a special privilege was announced for all contributors, whereupon their number rose to nearly 100%.

3. In a liberal, democratically oriented girls' camp, self-government and freedom from a structured program were stressed as goals in operation. An annual evening operetta, with a small entrance fee, was to be presented to members of the camp and visitors. The proceeds were to be contributed to a campership for foreign students, which the girls almost unanimously approved. A group of fifteen-year-old campers who had already attended the dress rehearsal decided not to attend the actual performance. They were informed that there was no obligation

to attend, but since no other activity had been provided for the evening, they would have to go to bed right after supper. The camp director was genuinely shocked by the suggestion that she was trying to force the girls to make a contribution to the fund, insisting that a realistic lack of supervision necessitated this course, even though there were innumerable facilities for quiet, unsupervised activities in which girls of this age took part on many evenings.

4. The faculty leader asked a group of university graduate students to pick a subject for a seminar. He then countered their choice with various "suggestions" of his own until the group fell silent. The leader then expressed satisfaction that "we are all agreed" on the topic he had suggested.

5. An overworked candidate in analytic training objected to presenting a continuous case unless he received credit for supervision. The seminar leader, who had difficulty finding time to supervise the case, chided him for a "poor attitude" and was completely unaware that his criticism was a subtle form of coercion.

Many behavioral and emotional disturbances in children can be traced at least in part to such manipulations by adults who are important to them. An honest, positive relationship with even one teacher may be the basis of vitally important reidentifications for a child. Conversely, hypocritical attitudes encountered in the school system may reinforce whatever tendencies a child may have derived from his previous experience to be hostile and distrustful of all authority figures. Adults also suffer from the need to be indirect, if for no other reason than that their professional or parental effectiveness in dealing with children is impaired.

Adults cannot always control behavior motivated by unconscious attitudes without professional help for themselves, but they can be made aware of acting in a way which negates their conscious intention. Sometimes even this degree of awareness will result in behavior less damaging to the child. In any case, if alerted to the damaging effect, adults can be taught to avoid the temptation to practice little tricks and evasions to control children under the illusion of giving freedom. Consultants working with staff members in many agencies—particularly with school personnel, administrators, teachers, guidance workers, nurses, secretaries, and everyone else in direct contact with the children—must make their consultees aware of the degree to which they use euphemisms, evasions, and "protective" deception of children in their ordinary methods of operation.

CHAPTER V

ENVIRONMENTAL SOURCES OF INTERPERSONAL STRESS

If a community psychiatrist acting as consultant to an agency or institution is to be fully effective, he must evaluate the total setting in which the staff and clients interact. A person's surroundings at any particular moment have an impact on him. Before a person's behavior can be evaluated, his reactions to stress imposed by factors in the immediate environment must be distinguished from behavior motivated by deep-seated intrapsychic conflicts or by conflicts in other parts of his life.

It is axiomatic that an agency itself becomes the immediate environment of the client and that the client's reaction to representatives of the agency may reduce or increase the stress upon him—which, in turn, will affect the way the client functions within the setting. From the moment of his first application, the client is faced with a new social situation destined to have considerable impact on him, no matter what other forces from home or work impinge on him. Forces within the immediate work situation also affect the attitudes of agency staff members, attitudes which are a significant factor in the client's environment. The consultant to an agency has an obligation to understand the sources of stress acting on the staff and clients in a particular setting at a particular moment and to consider what part this stress plays in the client's problem.

The consultant also can obtain sociological data as a by-product of his clinical service. Every agency or institution has certain characteristics related to the nature of its structure and function. Predictable patterns of interaction develop under certain circumstances between staff members themselves, and between these staff members and other people (administrators, relatives of clients, members of the general public) who feel that their own interests are either promoted or impeded by the agency's work. Tension in the personnel, created by forces operating within or upon the agency, will inevitably have an impact on the client and will be reflected in his behavior. Thus by observing how clients behave, and how the attitudes of the professional staff affect them, the consultant can obtain information on sources of stress common to a particular kind of agency.

As an example, I should like to demonstrate the sources of interpersonal stress I observed while conducting in-service training with staff members of day care centers for the children of working mothers and with teachers in several parent-participating nursery schools.

The day care centers were financed by appropriations renewed yearly through a vote of the state legislature. While under a common administrator and supervisor, each center served a different area of the city and a different population group; eligibility was limited to low-income families except in cases where the working mother was a school teacher or nurse. Although all centers were presumably interracial, one served a predominantly negro district, while another was located in a segment of the city populated largely by middle- and upper-middle-class married university students.

Head teachers in the different schools varied greatly in personality, background, and training. Although they were all experienced and competent in handling children, their methods varied considerably. Each teacher was allowed reasonable autonomy in setting up policies for running her school, and her authority was backed by the administration except in unusual circumstances. Each was placed in a district where her specific capabilities would be most effective and appreciated by the population served. She remained constantly in charge of the same school, while assistant teachers were often rotated from one center to another according to needs of the overall program. Each head teacher had four or five assistants, depending on the size of the group at any particular period.

The parent-participating nursery schools were part of an adult-education program financed, administered, and supervised under the local public school system. For the most part, they were located in or near the elementary schools and offered service only to the children of mothers enrolled for credit in nursery-education classes. A child could remain in the school only if the mother met certain requirements, including participation in the nursery school as an assistant under the supervision of a trained head teacher one morning each week, and strict attendance at one evening class each month in which the head teacher taught principles of child development and demonstrated books, music or play materials suitable for the age group. As part of the teaching in this class, a case study of each child's progress in the school came up for discussion at least once, and the child's mother was expected to take part in the discussion.

The group of children remained more or less fixed during the school year (with occasional newcomers or dropouts), but a different group of mothers assisted the teacher each day. An attempt was made to have the same mothers participate on the same days each week, but constant substitutions took place among them. On at least one day every week, each child had his own mother as a teacher. All of these factors had some part in difficulties that occurred at one time or another.

The staff of each day care center, and the group of head teachers from all the parent-participating schools, each met monthly with the consultant. The administrator of each program frequently attended these meetings, often playing an important role in implementing plans suggested in the discussions. Members were encouraged to bring up any subject that they wanted. In the vast majority of cases, material was first presented in the form of questions about disturbed behavior exhibited by a child or parent, with discussion then branching out in many directions. The consultant found few instances in which the teachers did not have knowledge and skills adequate to handle the child's problem once the source of immediate pressure upon a child was clearly defined.

The stress which produced disturbed behavior in a child was often created by his unconscious perception of adult anxiety or by the fact that an adult had displaced onto him feelings aroused in an interaction with someone else in the environment. These displaced reactions from previously unrecognized pressures upon a member or members of the staff were caused by some aspect of the administrative setup, by staff relationships, or by the nature of interactants in the school itself (an aspect of the social structure which is common to all nursery schools of the same type). Definition of sources of stress among all interactants was a major part of the consultant's clinical role in helping the staff to improve their functioning.

The chart (see p. 83) shows the interactants in a nursery school. The teacher, the child, and other children are present in every school. The child's mother and other mothers are physically present in the classroom only at parent-participating schools, but they are always important background figures who have some kind of relationship to the teacher (even if the relationship is one of avoidance) and often have contact with one another either in their community life or as they meet coming and going with their children. More than one teacher is present in most nonparticipating schools, while the larger community may be a very tangible presence in any school administered by a public agency.

In omitting the child's father from the diagram of important interactants, I did not intend to minimize his importance to the child, particularly in terms of his impact on the child's mother. The father is, however, seldom present in a nursery school environment, even though in some programs he is included in the didactic sessions. Whenever a father for any reason takes an active part in any nursery school program, he is a valuable asset. A whole book could be written about the need for more male figures in early childhood education.

The following cases have been chosen to illustrate disturbing interactions attributable to the nature of the environmental structure.

PUBLIC AGENCY PROGRAMS

Public opinion is a potent source of stress upon both administration and staff members in a nursery school program administered by an agency which is publicly financed. This is particularly true in programs which are specifically reviewed at regular intervals by legislative bodies who will determine their life or death by appropriating or withholding adequate funds. In such programs, the possibility of community disapproval may create chronic or acute anxiety

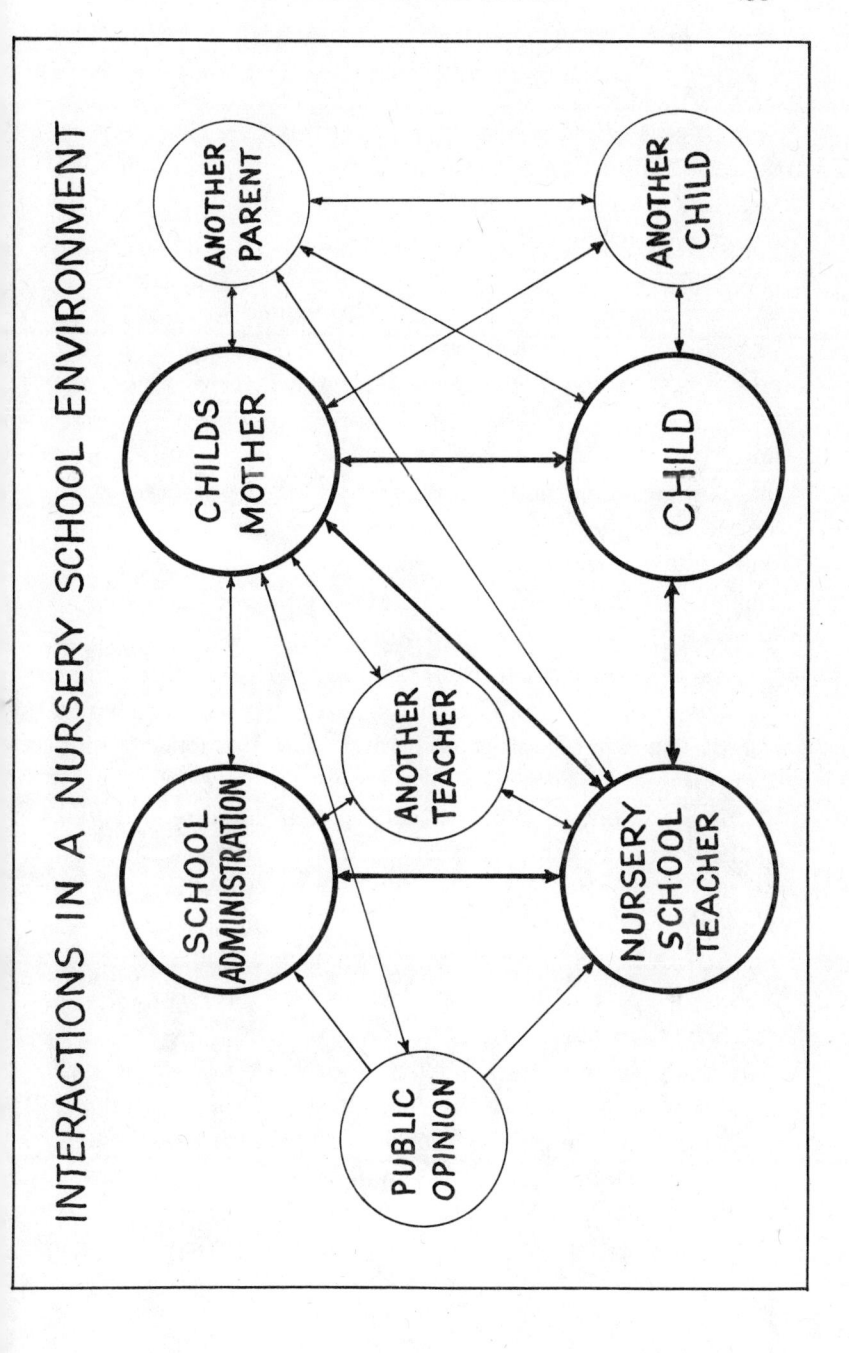

INTERACTIONS IN A NURSERY SCHOOL ENVIRONMENT

and may actually determine policy in the management of problems arising among the children.

Both administrators and staff of the day care centers were operating under such a burden of anxiety, although they were not aware of it. As voting time approached, teachers became highly sensitive to criticism from almost anyone, and especially sensitive to the possibility of bad publicity. In one school, the consultant was presented with the problem of a child who seemed to be aggressively endangering others. Discussion revealed the fact that several small, unusual accidents had recently occurred on the playground and that still earlier one child had been mildly injured by another. Gradually it emerged that the injured child came from the family of a teacher whose husband was politically active in the community. The mother had become excessively worried that serious accidents might occur in the school and had put pressure on the administrators who, in turn, became anxious and transmitted their anxiety to the teachers. The small accidents which happened shortly thereafter could clearly be traced to teacher tension and increased pressure on the children to "be careful" about everything they did. It can be seen that the behavior of the child originally presented stemmed from pressures on people in the environment quite remote from him, whose anxieties could be traced back directly to the way in which the school was financed. The triangle of significant interactants in this case (public opinion = administration = teacher) does not include the affected child.

In another consultation group with teachers from parent-participating schools, a new teacher said she was unable to handle the mounting tension in her group of mothers which was beginning to be felt by the children and reflected in uncontrollable behavior. A primary source of difficulty was one mother in the group, an aggressive, defiant woman, who was outspokenly contemptuous of the school program and who insisted on imposing her views upon the group. Although supported by all the other mothers in an unusually intelligent group, the young teacher, starting out in her first assignment in charge of a school, was thoroughly intimidated and became indecisive in directing the handling of problems which arose among the children. Since the disturbing mother scrupulously fulfilled technical requirements for participation, there seemed no way to resolve the situation. Discussion revealed clearly that the teacher's anxiety stemmed mainly from fear of this woman's status and influence in the community as wife of a prominent psychiatrist. Only emphatic encouragement from both consultant and administrator enabled the teacher to assert her authority and reestablish the other mothers' confidence in her capacity to supervise the school program. Again the interactional triangle (public opinion = mother = teacher) does not include the misbehaving children.

Eligibility requirements can cause problems; in fact, they were responsible for stirring up the mother's original antagonism in the case mentioned above. This woman was already well-informed on most subjects taught in the school and was on her second round of participation after completing the course with an older child. She had personal reasons for wanting her children in that particular school, and she was participating more or less against her will in order to obtain benefits for them. Regardless of her underlying personality problems and unpleasant ways of expressing frustration, her complaints were not without basis in fact when viewed from the standpoint of repeaters. Much veiled hostility by participating mothers can be traced to the fact that they are in the adult-education program only to obtain a good, relatively low-cost nursery school experience for their children, and not because they themselves value the educational experience. Various kinds of reaction by children result from the atmosphere created by such a situation. Here the triangle is administration = mother = teacher.

Major differences in theoretical orientation of different teachers in the same school are apt to occur in public agency programs where personnel are employed by the overall agency and may be rotated to different schools. Schools in different areas of the city have distinct problems depending on the demands and expectations of a particular parent group as well as on the ideas of an individual head teacher. Even an excellent assistant may be a misfit in a certain school and react accordingly. If, for instance, an assistant teacher is taken from a school where fairly permissive attitudes have prevailed and put into a more autocratically run school, she may feel overt opposition to the policies in her new school and the conflict may activate more deep-seated authority problems, which would not create difficulties in another setting. This kind of situation is less likely to occur in a private program where teachers are hired specifically for an individual school and chosen for attitudes consistent with its policies.

In a day care center with an almost equally balanced white and Negro population, the staff presented for consultation a Negro child who was prone to "pick fights." The whole staff was uneasy, a Negro teacher defensive for the child, and the head teacher defensive for the school. Discussion revealed that playground fights had recently been increasing between Negro and white children, although there had previously existed a high degree of successful integration. It became obvious to the consultant that an explosive relationship between the head teacher and her Negro assistant was creating a state of racial tension in the school which was perceived in some way and acted out by the children.

Personal insecurities on both sides, activated by differences in training and experience, lay at the heart of this problem, which was eventually solved only by an administrative decision to change the assistant teacher's placement. The head teacher had had many years of experience in work with preschoolers and had been remarkably successful in handling children and their parents intuitively. She was, however, somewhat defensive about a lack of formal training, and for this reason ran her school autocratically, making most of the important decisions without consulting her staff. Both Caucasian and minority group teachers had accepted this structuring, feeling that it gave them support in a rather touchy community climate. Into the setting, however, came a young, well-trained and intellectually gifted Negro teacher who had previously worked at a school with a more liberal atmosphere where her creative gifts were appreciated. Her own anxiety caused her to believe there was a racial basis for the head teacher's attitude. This feeling began to influence her objectivity about the school's special problems, and made her openly hostile and scornful of what she termed "old-fashioned" disciplinary handling by other personnel. Tension rose in the school as defensiveness increased in both women. When, as a result of the consultation, the young assistant was returned to her old school, interracial fights decreased as if by magic. In this triangle (administration = teacher = teacher), as usual, the disturbed children do not appear.

PARENT-PARTICIPATION PROGRAMS
(PUBLIC OR PRIVATE)

Any nursery school program in which parents are a part of the school environment has a special social situation. I will not discuss here the more-or-less overt reactions of mothers and their own children to each other when the mother's role is changed, since these are anticipated and usually well understood by teachers.

Displaced feelings onto a child or children, aroused by an adult's interaction with another person are less visible, although not much less common. Interaction between two mothers may affect the relationship of one of them to the teacher or to one of their children. A teacher's concern for one child may arouse hostility in the mother of another, or the relationship between two children may create conflict for the mother of one. Whenever any adult's feeling about another person affects her relationship to a child, her ability to be objective and to take an undistorted view of the child's behavior is impaired and the child will react in some way to the distortion.

For instance, in one school two mothers were antagonistic to each other because of matters unrelated to the school. One, according to the teachers, was "the most cooperative mother in the group, gentle with the children and creative in the program." The teacher's obvious liking for this woman aroused anxiety in the other, whose own motivation to cooperate deteriorated. When the uncooperative mother's child was attacked by the "good" mother's child, the teacher irrationally misperceived the incident, presenting the "bad" mother's child to the consultant in such a distorted way that the true situation became obvious to the whole group. It required strong pressure by teachers from the other schools to convince this teacher that the child she had seen as victim was actually the attacker. Here again the interactional triangle (mother = mother = teacher) does not include the child.

In another case, the teacher, who was known to be fond of a dainty, attractive two-and-a-half-year-old girl, protected her from aggressive hugging by a large four-year-old boy. The boy's mother felt him to be a victim of discrimination, losing sight of the fact that what she was interpreting as "normal masculine interest" on the part of her own child was largely due to insecurity with boys his own age and size. Subtle, uncooperative acts directed against the teacher threatened the morale of the whole school. The teacher, who presented this situation in terms of general difficulties in protecting small children from larger ones, had remained unaware of the source for increasing tension in the group of children. The interactional triangle is another child = mother = teacher.

Two four-year-olds were fast friends for a while and then split up as four-year-olds frequently do. One child soon made new friends and became an active member of his age group. The other felt lost and rejected, responding in whiny behavior that made him unpopular with his peers. His mother, repressing awareness of her anxiety about his regression, directed hostility toward the former playmate. Her frequent misinterpretations of his normally aggressive liveliness created anxiety in the child, who became uncooperative with all adults except the teacher and his own mother. He was presented to the group of teachers as an example of "mysterious and unusual selective behavior." Here the triangle does include the child as interactant, since feelings directed against him were aroused by his relationship to another child, even though the feelings on the adult's part were irrational. Here the triangle is another child = child = mother.

The child is also involved in the triangle of the following case (mother = mother = child) in which a mother's feeling about a child's father were again directed specifically toward a child, who reacted directly with hostility toward her. This mother, who held a high professional degree, had strong feelings about the status and rights of women. The affected child's father, an aggressively imperious Latin American, made no secret of his feeling that women should be confined to church and kitchen. The little boy himself, a charmer with snappy black eyes and curly hair, greatly enjoyed the adulation of the small female population. Everything that the mother hated and feared about derogatory attitudes of men toward women she saw in this child's play relationships with little girls. Every day on which she participated, a crisis involving this child had the school in an uproar, although on other days nobody had any trouble with him. The teacher who presented this case was aware of this woman's hostility toward the boy, but did not recognize it as a displaced reaction.

NONPARTICIPATION PROGRAMS (PUBLIC OR PRIVATE)

The influence of a teacher's feeling about a child's mother is always important in her attitude toward the child, although sometimes irrational elements are stronger than usual. A teacher may displace either positive or negative feelings toward the mother onto him or, if she has a child of her own, may identify with some aspect of the mother-child relationship and misperceive the mother's relationship to her child in terms of her own experiences. In any case, feelings about the child's mother may impair a teacher's objectivity about the child's problem. I shall give one example to illustrate how feelings about the parent affect a teacher's evaluation of the child's need and how conflict between the value systems held by parent and school may affect a child's capacity to function in the school. Here again the interactional triangle (teacher = mother = child) includes the child.

A pathetically disturbed three-year-old boy worried all the teachers in a day care center. He showed massive anxiety about all bodily excretions, often becoming panicky if he had a runny nose, and was terrified of wet or slimy materials of any sort. Teachers reported him as the only child they had ever seen who wiped his penis after urinating. The mother was, of course, compulsive about cleanliness, dressed him in starched pastel suits, and was extremely critical both of him and of the school if she found him dirty at the end of a day. The teachers unanimously resented her attitude and reacted to the child with exaggerated sympathy. As soon as the mother left, they dressed him in old jeans. At day's end, they carefully washed him, put back the immaculate clothing, and returned him unsullied to his mother. This might have been useful to the child if they had not gone further. During the day, he was actively encouraged to play with finger paint, clay and mud in the hope that familiarity with these materials, produced under sympathetic guidance, would decrease his fears. Instead of responding to this "therapy" by improving, the child became violently hostile to the teachers and acted so destructively that it eventually became necessary to remove him from the school. Inconsistent handling by two groups of people with grossly discrepant values created too much anxiety for this boy to master.

One more triangle (teacher = teacher = child) needs little elaboration, since it is a variation on the themes already mentioned. When two teachers in a school disagree about a personal or professional matter, there may be an impact on a child in the school even if he is in no way involved in the disagreement. If, for instance, two teachers dislike each other, and a child is fond of one, the other may dislike him. I have mentioned elsewhere that in this kind of situation, teachers feel extremely guilty, recognizing the irrationality of their feelings about the child but being unaware of its real source.

PRIVATE AGENCY PROGRAMS

Privately operated nursery schools, whether parent-participating or not, administered by a board of directors which is often composed of the mothers themselves, have many of the same problems described above, except for those attributed to outside pressure from the general public. They also have a problem which may exist in any kind of school but is less common where mothers themselves do not have much influence on the formation of administrative policy. Private schools are apt to attract parents with fairly similar educational values, the teachers being chosen to run the school in accordance with those values. Gross discrepancies in method among different teachers rarely occur, since those who do not share the school's value system do not remain. Parents may to some extent become educated by their teachers, usually accepting guidance by trained professionals in developing their policies. However, since they are themselves in a position to hire or fire, mothers can exert considerable pressure on the teachers who do not conform to their own views. An influential mother with ideas about how certain things should be run, even when the other mothers do not agree, may create anxiety in the teacher, who may feel it necessary to act contrary to her own conviction. Whenever a teacher (or anyone else) tries to carry out a policy she doesn't believe in, the impact is always felt by the children. Insincerity in an adult is sensed on some level of consciousness and causes confusion in the child's perception of reality or distrust of the person who is trying to fool him. Conflicts between what a teacher is consciously doing and what she preconsciously wishes to do may also result in "masked authoritarianism," which has already been discussed in some detail.

I could cite many examples, but will mention only a few that I found to be common to all nursery schools. In many programs, certain activities are supposed to be "voluntary," such as midmorning snacks or participation in group games during a "free-play period." Nevertheless the adults feel for one reason or another that the child *should* undertake these "voluntary" activities. If he refuses his juice, or prefers to play alone in a corner, the staff may feel anxious or be inconvenienced because of a shortage in supervisory personnel. Instead of just telling the child what he is expected to do, the adult tries to persuade him that he "wants" his juice, etc. Often the child ends up actually thinking he made a choice to do what the teacher wants, but on some level he knows he was manipulated into it. If he is constantly manipulated by little tricks (some of which are taught in professional training schools), he may become uncooperative. This is the source of much "mysterious" hostility on the part of small children.

SUMMARY

In this section I have discussed the fact that in every kind of agency certain aspects of its social structure may be related to unexplained behavior of staff and clients. Methods by which the agency is financed, the form of administration and supervision, whether it is public or private, the clientele served and eligibility requirements, as well as the composition and responsibilities of its staff all have some kind of impact which may be reflected in attitudes displayed at any moment, regardless of underlying personality factors of individuals which may be contributing to the reaction. These factors, common to all similar agencies, can be discovered as a by-product of clinical consultation with agency staff and provide data to facilitate consultation with staff groups in comparable settings.

CHAPTER VI

ANALYSIS OF AN IN-SERVICE TRAINING PROGRAM FOR PUBLIC HEALTH NURSES

The following description of an in-service training program for public health nurses is taken from a previously published report covering the four-year period between October 1953 and June 1957 (Parker, 1958). During that time, a psychiatric consultant met for two hours once a month with each group of four to six nurses in a total of 96 meetings and had 16 separate sessions with supervisory staff. After each session, informal notes were recorded in various degrees of detail. Data, although compiled in an unstructured way, give a fairly comprehensive picture of the ways in which each session was conducted and the subjects covered.

Analysis of the material offers information about the consultant's objectives in handling each session and the kinds of activity employed in directing discussions. I shall first describe these aspects of the consultant's role and follow with an analysis of subject matter presented by the nurses, their stated reasons for presenting individual problems, and the consultant's view of the problem presented—which may or may not have coincided with that of the nurses themselves.

CONSULTANT'S OBJECTIVES

Almost all the meetings were recorded in sufficient detail to permit retrospective estimation of the consultant's probable objectives in each session. Two major categories emerge. In one, the consultant was primarily engaged in influencing the process or content of group thinking. This was accomplished partly through demonstrating methods of examining a problem, estimating the relevance of data, and calling upon the group for previous work experience with related situations. Partly it was done through attempts to expand the scope of group thinking and break down stereotypes, changing emphasis from surface to more underlying problems, pointing out controversial issues, or challenging assumptions and exploring factors in an individual case which distinguished it from similar cases. Intellectual horizons were widened and attitudes changed by explaining motivations, giving information on psychological mechanisms, and commenting on differing social structures, customs, and attitudes. By pointing out aspects of a particular nurse's involvement which impeded her objectivity, the consultant often influenced ways in which a whole group viewed similar problems.

Secondly, a major objective was to reduce individual or group anxiety, either directly or by implication. Guilt over emotional reactions was relieved by allowing ventilation, showing universality, and expressing nonjudgmental attitudes. Threats to a nurse's status or sensibilities were reduced by explaining patient motivation, increasing pride in the nurse's actual performance, or encouraging intellectualization about shocking subject matter to hasten desensitization of group members to it. Conflicts over jurisdiction were relieved by sharing responsibility for decisions and helping set limits to a nurse's assumption of problems. Discussion was purposely deflected from attention to a nurse's own emotional reaction when such a focus seemed contraindicated.

In a sense, of course, every session was a demonstration of methods for investigating problems, and reduction of anxiety was always an assumed goal. Nevertheless, at certain times, the consultant's attention was primarily focused on one or another of these objectives.

CONSULTANT'S ACTIVITY

The consultant used five forms of activity in carrying out these objectives. One involved *encouraging the group to explore* certain aspects of the material, observable patient behavior, the effect of nurses' feelings on a specific type of problem, or factors which induced a nurse to assume responsibility for a particular problem. During this kind of activity, a consultant inevitably instructs workers in techniques of interviewing, even if he does not do so explicitly. Although he may openly point out the value of examining individual experience for possible answers to general questions, encourage people to obtain the whole picture before passing judgment on isolated aspects of it, or comment on the importance of paying attention to the underlying as well as the presenting problem, he transmits these concepts for the most part by example, employing the method constantly himself. By helping a group examine their own experience, or by pointing out aspects of a problem that has been overlooked, the consultant teaches workers to use the same methods in helping their patients or clients reach decisions.

Other activities involved *interpreting meanings or implications, discussing general principles, delivering abstract information,* or *handling immediate emotional reactions* of individuals or groups.

Group exploration of various types of problems gives the consultant a significant opportunity to redirect channels of thinking and expand intellectual horizons. In the course of in-service training with groups of workers, he can introduce many new ideas and call attention to many fallacies or stereotypes and assumptions which are often taken for granted by large segments of the population without much thought. An important objective of in-service training by a psychiatrist or psychologist is to open up new fields of knowledge and experience for workers in other professions, giving them a broadened perspective on how their role fits into the larger social structure and making them proud of the impact that individuals doing the ordinary work of their profession can have upon the emotional growth and stability of other human beings in their society.

Group exploration of patient behavior and symptomatology in order to answer a nurse's question about her own functioning may be illustrated by discussion of a fourteen-year-old diabetic boy who refused to come to the nurse's office for midmorning and afternoon milk prescribed by his physician. Should the nurse force him to come; and if so, how? Group members focused on the boy's possible reasons for refusal, with the consultant throwing in an idea that his sensitivity about being conspicuous might arise not only from feelings about the disease but from other feelings of inferiority displaced onto it. With this in mind, the boy's total functioning was examined. Other areas in which he showed anxiety were uncovered. The group then went on to consider possible remedies, and suggested that to spare the boy teasing about being a "milksop," his physician be asked to prescribe milk substitutes for him to eat in the classroom. The nurse's anxiety decreased as she saw chances for constructive action, and gained a better understanding of the boy's "stubborn" behavior.

Exploration of a nurse's feelings and their effect on a specific problem may be handled either by making her aware of unconscious feelings or by showing how similar feelings affect the functioning of public health nurses in general. Once a nurse is aware of how her reaction complicates handling of a problem, group discussion and support, supplemented by support from the consultant, are usually all that is required.

A nurse complained that pressure of routine duties prevented her from spending enough time in helping sick patients with the "emotional aspects of their problem." Group members focused immediately on the concept that her interest in being a "counselor" prevented the nurse from realizing that in regressed states of severe illness, the amount of time spent with a patient is of far less importance to him than the quality of feeling expressed by a nurse while carrying out her routine duties. The nurse had not been aware of her need to see herself as a counselor until her colleagues pointed it out, but the discussion relieved her anxiety about the performance of her functions.

With some anxiety, one nurse presented the case of a boy considered "odd" who complained of deafness not demonstrated by tests. The child's mother seemed psychotic to the nurse, who asked whether the boy could be removed from his home. In this case, the nurse's anxiety was related to stereotyped ideas of psychosis which had ominous implications to her, irrespective of the type, degree, or manner in which it was expressed. The consultant brought this out in group discussion and showed how the stereotype prevented the nurse from judging whether the boy's difficulties warranted any action at all. Some information was given on the widespread existence of ambulatory schizophrenia and the relatively good functioning of many people with varying types and degrees of psychosis. The group discussed the boy's symptom in relation to evidence of otherwise good functioning and agreed that observable aspects of the mother-child relationship indicated warmth. Once the nurse was aware that her fears related to a stereotype and not to the patient, she was able to evaluate his symptoms from a different perspective.

Another nurse reported that a child's mother had expressed dissatisfaction with the physician to whom she had been referred and asked advice from the nurse. The nurse felt reluctant to make a second referral to a physician but also felt incompetent to give the desired advice. Although, in the consultant's opinion, the main source of this nurse's indecision lay in unconscious guilt for her competitiveness with the physician, this point was not raised for group discussion. Other nurses pointed out that she was trying to solve the problem herself, rather than helping the mother understand what kind of help she needed. The main focus of discussion then became the importance of helping patients find their own solutions to problems. The group's explanation that the nurse had too much need to "do something" for the patient was much more ego-acceptable and far more useful to her than an uncovering of her unconscious conflict would have been.

A minority group nurse realized that in attempting to comfort a physically handicapped child who complained of being "picked on" by a teacher, she had actually provoked him to feel persecuted. Recognizing her overidentification with the child, she nevertheless felt helpless and feared repercussions from school personnel. The group immediately came to her defense with accounts of similar experiences they had had and helped decrease her anxiety by offering constructive suggestions for handling any criticism that might arise.

Admission by the consulting psychiatrist that he and other physicians also have "unacceptable" reactions in the course of their work may enable workers from other professions to confess feelings they might otherwise withhold in shame. Sometimes such an admission will start a whole chain of confessions in a group, resulting in a reduction of general anxiety. Support by a group is always the most valuable type of reassurance to workers, particularly when it is strengthened by support from the consultant, and ego-alien attitudes can be tolerated or dispelled by knowledge that they exist in other "respectable" professional people.

One important activity of a consultant is to accept responsibility for setting clear limits to a worker's involvement with a case. Conflicts over their jurisdiction and the degree of desirable participation in a case are sources of concern to public health nurses and other workers who sometimes feel called upon to assume responsibility that really belongs somewhere else and who, after a little exposure to psychological concepts, are sometimes tempted to try administering a form of psychotherapy to patients who confide intimate details of their lives. Willingness on a consultant's part to share responsibility for group decisions permits workers to explore new approaches to old problems without fear of getting in "over their depth."

A nurse's indecision about taking responsibility may be illustrated by a situation in which a school nurse was under pressure from the principal to "get (a child) back to school." The family insisted the child could not tolerate school because of factors related to his psychiatric treatment, but the psychiatrist had refused to "abuse confidentiality" by writing an official excuse. The nurse wanted to know whether she had a responsibility to enforce attendance in the absence of a medical excuse. The consultant supported a group decision that problems of this kind fell under the jurisdiction of the principal rather than the nurse. She was assured that refusal to assume responsibility would be upheld by health department officials and that conflict with the school principal would be handled by her supervisor.

Roughly half the time, suggestions for management of cases came from members of the group who had had similar experiences, while the consultant only added additional ideas after the group had exhausted theirs. Sometimes a group needed new perspective on a problem. For instance, one nurse expressed guilt for punitive feelings toward a woman who neglected her aged father. After both the group and the consultant had stressed the universality of anger at "mean" people, the consultant added that it was nevertheless sometimes necessary for a professional person to discharge a hostile reaction somewhere else in order to attain a goal with the patient. The nurse was encouraged to abandon her retaliatory behavior toward the woman, by demonstration that such behavior worked against her goal of helping the old father.

Showing alternatives to unsuccessful methods of handling a problem and indicating fallacies in a decision without being critical of the original effort converts feelings of discouragement and failure into a renewed interest in finding solutions. When group members see that talking about their feelings and reactions leads to positive resolution of a difficulty without subjecting them to fear of blame, they voluntarily suggest examining their methods of handling cases.

In many sessions, emphasis was to some extent diverted from a specific problem to the general principles involved. For example, in discussing the case of a mother who recently had arrived from a foreign country and who complained bitterly to the nurse about detrimental effects of American culture on her child, the consultant pointed out that cultural conflicts often mask underlying personal problems. Instead of pursuing this, however, the group preferred to talk in general terms about the conflicts of second-generation American children and children of minority groups. Although the nurse's difficulty was due to lack of interviewing skill and an inability to discover the mother's real problem, the group's interest lay in a subject stimulated by the case.

Quite a few discussions of general principles concerned problems that a public health nurse has in performing her function. A nurse complained of having to interview venereal disease patients for contacts. She expressed a "horror of such people" and said she couldn't be comfortable talking to them. Discussion was deflected from her personal reaction to venereal disease patients specifically and turned toward general public health situations which arouse similar feelings.

Many general problems fall under such headings as "reactions common to certain developmental stages or cultural groups." For example, two nurses in one group reported that their own ten-year-old boys had become uncommunicative with the family and wanted to know whether something was "wrong." Consultant and group members shared their knowledge of normal preadolescent behavior, and in both cases, specific cases were answered in general terms.

While undertaking to evaluate certain routine duties, a nurse asked what kind of information about behavior and emotional difficulties should be entered on a child's permanent health record. Group members expressed reluctance to "pin a label" on children, and the consultant cited theory that transient phases of behavior may become permanent as "negative identity" if a child receives public recognition as a "bad boy." The group answered the specific question by talking over the theory.

Dealing with anxiety or hostility expressed by an individual or by the group has been a primary activity in relatively few sessions. Supportive reaction by the group consisted of sharing the feeling, generalizing the problems, or explaining behavior arousing the reaction, with suggestions for management. The group defended a nurse whenever she expressed a feeling while showing obvious signs of anxiety, or whenever a group projected anxiety onto her because of the nature of a problem she presented for discussion.

Abstract information was given by the consulting psychiatrist on only a few occasions, almost always in a lecture on material raised in a case presentation. Once, after a case involving sexual aberration was anxiously presented before one group of new nurses, the consultant gave a lecture to all the nurses on various sexual problems that might be encountered on the job, since it was obviously necessary to fill gaps in the basic professional education of these workers.

SUBJECT MATTER

Topics raised for discussion by these groups of public health nurses fell into three major categories.

1. *General problems of understanding or handling.* This included such subjects as relevant cultural and environmental factors, use of community facilities or procedures which aid the nurse's function, types of psychological disturbances or mechanisms and their uses, behavior and symptoms of patients, problems encountered by all public health nurses, feelings common to all public health nurses on the job, questions or criticisms of department policy, and general principles of public health nursing.

2. *Problems encountered by a nurse in some aspect of her work.* These included problems of handling requests for service, problems of carrying out assignments, expressions of feeling about some aspect of the job, or expressions of a personal problem.

3. *Deviant attitudes and behavior or symptoms of patients.* A nurse presented a case either because she wanted help

with understanding and handling the problem, to express an emotional reaction of her own, or to mention the effect of the patient's deviance on people in his environment.

Most of the general topics and a high proportion of the case material related to the problems of children or parents. This may have been due to the fact that the consultant had been a pediatrician and was known to have a particular interest in this area, but I think it also reflected a genuine concern among nurses for this segment of their patient population. It may also have reflected a tendency to deny anxiety about the problems of a geriatric population which occupies a high proportion of public nursing time.

NURSES' REASONS FOR PRESENTING SUBJECT

Although in most cases nurses first presented subject matter in the form of a wish for information about patients rather than admitting that they themselves had a problem, the phrasing of most questions indicated a desire on the nurse's part either to carry out her role more effectively, avoid criticism and justify attitudes, or to express an emotional reaction to problems and attitudes encountered on the job.

What nurses wanted most from the consultant was support and clarification of their role, and primary focus was on their own functioning. They seemed to feel great guilt for any hostile reactions toward patients and sought rationalizations for them, but they also wanted to understand better how the motivations and feelings of patients prevented the nurses from doing a good job and getting satisfaction from it.

Certain types of general topics recurred among groups of nurses. Most frequent were situations involving parents who do not meet school requirements, difficulties in handling dirty patients, justification for requesting deviation from school routines for the good of individual children, difficulties in making objective evaluations in the case of individual children who might need free lunch, and difficulties in evaluating need for reduced home nursing care fees.

Reasons given for presenting cases were often phrased in terms of "How can I change the attitude, behavior, or motivation of the patient so that he will conform to my standard?" or "How far shall I go in assuming responsibility?" The emotional reactions expressed were anxiety, frustration, or resentment of the problem or toward the attitudes of others concerning a nurse's function. Many cases were presented in a way that clearly indicated a desire to avoid criticism for, or to justify, these emotional reactions.

Some cases brought up for discussion are described below, with a brief account of how they were handled.

A housing project inmate asked one nurse to help a neighbor with prenatal "emotional problems." The woman insisted on calling in her friend then and there, and the nurse talked to the "patient" with no specific indication that the woman herself wanted help. Although the "patient" was polite and agreed to a further appointment, she subsequently avoided the nurse's visit. The reason for presenting the case was given as a desire for advice on how to accomplish the follow-up visit. Group discussion pointed out that the difficulty arose because the nurse overlooked the need for patient motivation but centered primarily on explaining the patient's need to resist unsolicited service. Participants recommended dropping the case unless the woman herself indicated a wish to reopen it.

Another nurse expressed frustration because, although she had spent considerable time explaining the need for checkup to two people who had had contact with a tuberculosis patient, neither had kept the clinic appointments made for them. What had she done wrong, and what could she do to get these people in? The discussion was aimed at reducing her feeling of personal rejection and failure by pointing out various reasons why some patients avoid contact with health authorities.

A fifteen-year-old boy with severe asthma, who spent most of his school day in the nurse's office, did not want to be sent home but was only able to remain in class for short periods because his wheezing disturbed other students. The nurse wanted to know whether he should be sent home or encouraged to stay in class despite his symptoms. She admitted that prolonged listening to his labored breathing also made *her* uncomfortable, and the consultant felt she was attempting to justify a preconscious desire to get rid of him which violated her concept of the "right attitude" for a nurse. Discussion was, however, directed toward clarification of her difficulty in obtaining objective information on which to evaluate the problem.

A thirteen-year-old girl who sucked her thumb was described to one group by a nurse who had to write a report for the mental health clinic and wanted help in deciding what information to include. Discussion centered on the child's observable behavior, and the consultant explained implications of her symptoms.

A mother with germ phobia kept her child out of school whenever anyone in the class had even a mild cold. The nurse wanted clarification of her own responsibility for forcing conformity to school attendance requirements and asked what methods she could use to satisfy those requirements. The group concentrated on the idea that such a problem could only be solved by reaching the mother in a way that did not threaten her, and that school personnel are not always the most acceptable counselors in helping parents solve certain kinds of problems. During discussion it became clear that the person most apt to be acceptable as adviser to this mother was the parish priest, and the nurse was encouraged to enlist his aid. Explicitly, the nurse received advice on management of the case, but implicitly she was relieved of anxiety about her responsibility.

Germ phobia in a teacher caused her to usurp the nurse's prerogative for diagnosing contagious disease in her pupils. The nurse sought justification for "telling the teacher off," and received support from the group by assurance that "there's one of those in every school." Nurses who had had comparable experiences offered concrete suggestions for dealing with the situation without antagonizing the teacher.

A ninety-year-old man made lewd remarks to a nurse, commenting that she could "take it" because "nurses are free and easy." The nurse described her case in an explosive ventilation of anger tinged with amusement. The consultant brought up reasons for heightened sexuality in old men and the implications of this common finding for a nurse's job, implicitly attempting to reduce the group's anxiety over a hostile stereotype of nurses.

CONSULTANT'S OBSERVATIONS

Nurses' questions indicated their views on why a case presented problems. The consultant observed other reactions and motivations displayed unconsciously by the nurses which at times constituted a major obstacle to their solution of the problem described. Nurses' difficulties, as seen by the consultant, fell into three categories.

1. *Lack of techniques and skill* in interviewing or in evaluating data.

2. *Ignorance of psychic mechanisms and interpersonal processes.* This included devaluing a patient's motivation for learning and change, overlooking the need for a patient to solve his own problems, and failing to realize that a warm interpersonal relationship with a professional person can

help a patient even if it does not help the professional person reach her practical goal.

3. *Emotional reactions interfering with objective evaluation* of a problem. These included anxiety or hostility toward a patient or colleague who rejected the nurse's own value system, or toward people whose attitudes were a threat to the nurse's concept of her role; anxiety and hostility aroused by conflict between a nurse's sympathy for a patient and her responsibility to carry out policy or by awareness of ego-alien attitudes in herself; and instinctual anxiety activated by the nature of the material.

In the consultant's opinion, most difficulties reported by the nurses resulted to some degree from such loss of objectivity. Only occasionally did lack of skills or knowledge contribute in a major degree to the problem of any experienced nurse.

Lack of field experience was evident in the case presented by a young nurse just out of training and new to the department. On her first day as school nurse, she was asked for advice about handling a child's somatic problem which the mother said had an "emotional basis." The nurse, insecure about her knowledge in this area, suggested that the mother talk it over with someone "specially trained," whereupon the mother burst into tears and the nurse panicked. Older members of the group gave reassurance that her inability to help the mother was due to inexperience on the job, and discussion brought out ways of relieving such parental anxieties. The consultant added reasons why referral to a psychiatrist has such a frightening impact on certain people.

Lack of knowledge about psychopathology was a major cause of one nurse's inability to evaluate a mother's insistence that her eleven-year-old daughter was pregnant, despite numerous medical opinions and reassurance to the contrary. Group exploration of the nurse's observations brought to light several subtle evidences of unrecognized psychosis in the mother, which were pointed out and explained by the consultant.

In early meetings of several groups, nurses reported that asthma was a symptom frequently encountered in school children and requested information about the emotional factors involved and about the handling of such cases. The consultant offered some simple psychoanalytic theory regarding causation, but laid primary stress on the fact that ideas about emotional causation can be threatening to parents and that nurses should try to understand the kinds of problems an asthmatic child creates in a family.

Many emotional reactions interfering with a nurse's objectivity were caused by anxiety or conflict in the nurse aroused in response to behavior in patients or colleagues which deviated from middle-class mores. (Similar emotional reactions are experienced by a large number of people accustomed to regarding the behavior of lower socioeconomic groups as "undesirable.") For example, nurses were apt to condemn religious beliefs and practices that interfered with a child's adjustment to his school group; frequently nurses felt that children should be removed from "deviant" homes.

Unfamiliar emotional symptoms may arouse hostility if they are judged by stereotypes of "desirable" behavior and morality. One nurse indignantly presented the case of a "grossly neglectful" mother whose child was having emotional disturbances and severe academic difficulties resulting from spotty retinal degeneration. The mother refused to believe in the seriousness of his symptoms and would not allow transfer of the child to a sight-saving class. The nurse, although well oriented toward acceptance of the medical reality, was uninformed about psychological mechanisms by which a mother might deny to herself a child's disability.

Standards of a "Bohemian" college professor, whose child's clothing and habits of cleanliness did not meet school standards, aroused sharp criticism from nurses, even though the child was obviously not in any way disturbed or rejected by his group.

Nurses often expressed indignation and frustration at the difficulties encountered in trying to persuade members of cultural minorities or of foreign birth to change their dietary preferences in conformance with professional standards of nutrition. Health department personnel frequently have to be specifically taught to introduce important nutritional elements into "strange" diets without expecting people to alter their eating habits.

The consultant often had to ask, and to stress, the question "Who has the problem?" Is deviation from the accepted standards actually harmful to a patient, or does it only offend the sensibilities of school and health department personnel?

Almost half of the reactions interfering with objectivity involved hostile reactions to people whose attitudes threatened the nurse's concept of her role. These reactions were aroused by people who made the nurse feel helpless or ineffective by refusing service, by devaluating the nurse's position, or by endangering themselves and threatening the nurse's prestige or feeling of usefulness.

Anxiety over the attitudes of superiors or colleagues was exemplified by conscious resentment over what many nurses considered a misuse of their time in the schools. To be considered "a glorified truant officer" or a "putter-on of Bandaids" was anathema to many whose training had encouraged them to consider themselves teachers and counselors on matters of both physical and emotional health. Nurses put a high value on acceptance as part of a team dealing with "the whole child" and as members of school faculty with status equal to that of teachers. A superior or colleague who seemed to devalue them in this role was regarded with hostility.

The same reaction was felt toward patients who refused help or depreciated the nurse's function. For instance, a nurse called at the home of a professor whose seven-year-old child had been showing evidence of nervousness apparently related to pressures at home. The mother insisted that the child had plenty of play time and told the nurse "it was none of (her) business anyway." The nurse was doubly threatened—by the mother's refusal to accept her in the role of counselor and by her own feeling of insecurity in the school hierarchy, which only ambivalently supported her in this role. Tuberculosis patients, who frequently see the nurse as "interfering," also threaten a nurse's image of herself as a help and comfort.

Patients who endanger themselves and subject the nurse to possible criticism were the targets of considerable anger from nurses in the discussion groups. One visiting nurse had urged hospitalization of an aged diabetic who was careless about caring for himself but who wanted her to continue treating him at home. Consciously, the nurse was afraid for his safety; unconsciously she was also anxious to be rid of the responsibility. Assurance from the group that the old man got a feeling of security from being cared for in familiar surroundings changed her attitude toward the amount of time taken up in routine visits. As discussion progressed, she was able to see that, measured objectively, the patient's condition did not warrant forced hospitalization.

Among nurses, the "right attitude" for a nurse requires inhibition of conscious hostility toward a patient and precludes recognition of a wish to be rid of him even when they can openly acknowledge he is a nuisance. Instead of such feelings, nurses are apt to experience unconscious guilt reflected in feelings of helplessness or in unconscious expressions of hostility toward the patient. One group raised the question "How much should you knock yourself out to meet requests for bedside care at specific hours that are convenient for the patient but may complicate your work schedule?" From the discussion, it became apparent that if a patient's attitude is "demanding," the nurse is tempted to refuse his request no matter what the circumstances. When "demandingness" was interpreted as one way of expressing anxiety, a nurse often altered her view of reality factors at work in a particular case.

When a nurse's sympathy or empathy for an individual patient conflicts with her responsibility as representative of public authority, her ability to make decisions is impaired. Difficulty of this sort is intensified when a nurse harbors conscious or unconscious feelings of rebellion against personnel or policies of the agency she serves. One school nurse's plea for criteria upon which to determine a child's eligibility for free school lunch is an example of such conflict. She found it difficult to evaluate the case objectively because, on several grounds, she resented the school principal's instructions to "cut down the free lunch list." Rebellion against the policy stemmed from ideological and sociophilosophical disagreement with her school principal.

Instinctual anxiety is aroused in most public health nurses by certain types of subject matter, primarily that involving aberrant behavior or attitudes connected with sex or feces. Sometimes the anxiety is denied and displaced onto someone else like the school teacher. Often it is openly expressed, as in the case involving a seventy-year-old man who, after a partial stroke, exhibited constant sexual excitement and demanded that his cardiac wife submit to repeated acts of intercourse lasting "for hours." The whole group was thunderstruck! In another group, a comparable reaction was produced by description of an encopretic child who used his feces for ammunition against second-grade classmates. When this type of case was presented for discussion, the consultant usually tried to explain the symptoms and suggest definite corrective measures to the nurse faced with handling some aspect of the problem.

In high-morale groups, individual nurses were occasionally stimulated by the subject matter under discussion to introduce a personal problem. Invariably any nurse who did so received group support and reassurance. In the 10 years of my experience as a mental health consultant, no one ever brought before a group personal matters that were inappropriate in kind or degree even when individual or group anxiety ran high.

CHAPTER VII

ANALYSIS OF IN-SERVICE TRAINING SESSIONS WITH NURSERY SCHOOL PERSONNEL

In the following section I shall present detailed analyses of several sessions with each group of teachers in the three day care centers, attempting to illustrate concretely the ways in which a consultant's thinking and clinical evaluation of factors operating within a group affect the choice of his activity at each stage of discussion.

At the time chosen for this report, I had previously consulted for five years with all these groups and knew quite a bit about the individual personalities of group members, but I had been absent for a year working at the elementary grade levels. During my absence, no in-service training had been offered to day care or nursery school groups, and several teachers had been active in pressing the administration to reinstate a program for them.

The first few sessions following my return will be used, because they illustrate a variety of theoretical statements already made about factors which influence a consultant's initial methods of operation and ongoing choices of intervention. I had lost close touch with group members, and there were some new ones; so I needed to reevaluate the climate at each center, so to some extent I was faced with the problems encountered by a consultant coming for the first time to an agency. On the other hand, a previous working relationship with most of the teachers, a reputation for having been helpful before, and a knowledge within the group that I understood the general character of each school and its individual problems, had already established an atmosphere of confidence and group morale which eliminated some of the difficulties created by initial defensiveness in all participants when a new consultant starts with a group unaccustomed to in-service training.

I shall first give a brief description of the communities and clientele served by each center, significant personality characteristics of the teachers, and an evaluation of the physical plants. The account of each session will take, in chronological order, the comments and behavior of teachers (condensed, but essentially presented exactly as recorded immediately afterward), followed by the consultant's thoughts [in brackets] and comments in *italics*.

In presenting these sessions, I in no way intend to imply that the material was handled in the *only* way, or even in the *right* way. In my opinion, there can never be any one right way to handle any kind of material. Other consultants faced with the same situation would be struck by other aspects and would emphasize other points. I use the sessions merely to illustrate the kinds of questions that may be in the mind of a group leader during presentation of material for discussion and the way in which his own view of what is most relevant determines his course of action.

Center A is in the university section of town, serving for the most part children of students and educated middle-class working mothers. The head teacher, educated in child development and interested in psychoanalytic theory, carries out a policy of considerable permissiveness with regard to children's instinctual expressions. Assistant teachers, more psychologically sophisticated than those in other centers, include a few who have been in personal psychotherapy, and one or two who are definitely "Bohemian" in their attitudes. A few of the others might be described as motherly, old-fashioned types. Physical facilities are adequate both inside and out.

First Session after Consultant's Absence

    T. (Cordial welcome from all teachers, followed by an almost immediate declaration of magical expectations.)
    We always found that after talking a case over with you, things seemed to take care of themselves.
    C. [Why do they have to see me as practicing magic?]
    T. (Case presentation: An aggressive child who has been in school for a long time is about to move on to kindergarten. Teachers are worried about his ability to adjust and would like to refer the mother to a guidance facility, but they feel she is insecure and needs to deny that the child has a problem.)
    How shall we approach the subject with her?
    C. [The group seems to have regressed to a helpless, dependent level, demanding direct suggestions as though they had never used in-service training sessions. Before I went away, they were the best group of all in exploring problems for themselves and taking initiative with situations far more complicated than this.]
    T. The mother seems to be extremely sensitive to criticism. We think our suggestions have increased her own sense of inadequacy.
    C. [The group seems to be presenting its own problem. I must have threatened their own sense of adequacy or they wouldn't need to make me a

magician. Was it premature for me to leave? Maybe they carried on last year with a shaky independence that collapsed as soon as "mother came home." Did they act as helpless as they sound? What does it mean to them to have a consultant? Should I raise the question right now? It's too early. Better focus on the case instead of their feelings for the moment.]

What gives you the feeling that you can't talk to this mother about her child?

T. (Group says maybe they could if they felt sure of their ability to create a noncritical atmosphere. They discuss steps they might take to do this and end up feeling they can probably handle the situation.)

Second Session, One Month Later

T. The child we discussed last time was better the next day!

C. *That certainly was magic!* (Everyone laughs.)

[They obviously got something from discussing the problem that restored their perspective.]

T. Now we have another problem.

(Case presentation: A four-and-a-half-year-old child, who has been in the school two years, has not progressed as well as his parents hoped in learning English. The parents are Latin American students who will soon return to their own country. At first the child was very insecure, attaching himself to another child and imitating everything he did.)

That was while you were away, and we didn't know how to handle it. Now he does the same thing with another child, but in spite of the extreme imitation, he hasn't picked up the language. How can we help him progress faster?

C. [They are still on their own problem, telling me they tried to do everything the way I do, but it didn't help them internalize the method. Let's see if they are acting as helpless as they sound.]

How did you approach the problem?

T. (Group discusses the fact that at first they did nothing, recognizing that the child needed someone to cling to in a strange environment. Lately, however, they have gotten the feeling he doesn't need to as much and have taken several practical steps to encourage him in assuming independence. He is responding well, but still isn't fluent enough in English.)

C. [The teachers have obviously helped the child, who is improving. He no longer presents a real problem for the school, but the teachers are anxious because they want him to progress faster in becoming self-sufficient, just as they want to do themselves. Now that I have something constructive to say, I'll focus on their own attitude.]

You have done everything I could have thought of. Your feeling of helplessness seems out of proportion to your actual performance, and I'm wondering whether this has anything to do with my having left you last year.

T. (Group bursts into explosive laughter, saying they must have needed to show me how much they needed a consultant.)

C. *In what way is having a consultant so important to you?*

T. So many people think of nursery school teachers as glorified baby sitters. It's important to us to be thought capable of dealing with children's problems on a higher level. Also, the consultant is an important catalyst to our own thinking. While you were away, we tried holding meetings by ourselves to discuss problems, but they lacked inspiration.

C. *Before we stop, let's go back to the child we talked about last time. What do you think was involved in his dramatic improvement?*

T. Well, maybe it wasn't quite as dramatic as we implied, but after we talked about him, everyone felt friendlier to him, and he responded.

C. *Exit the magician!* (Everyone laughs.)

Center B is in a more racially mixed but still essentially middle-class district. The head teacher is young and well-trained. Assistant teachers are mostly older than she, more "comfortable" and less recently trained but eager to be professional. "Crises" frequently occur at this center on days scheduled for the session, which either necessitate cancellation or create confusion and interruptions. Physical facilities are cramped both indoors and out.

First Session after Consultant's Absence

A meeting of the nursery school staff, program administrator and consultant has been scheduled to include elementary school guidance personnel already working with the mother of a child to be presented. Although more disturbed than anyone previously admitted to a day care center for normal children, this three-year-old girl was accepted on a temporary basis because of special circumstances. The first in-service training session is to be used for discussing her diagnosis and considering whether she can be retained for the six months, pending transfer of the family to another community.

After initial explanation of circumstances surrounding the child's acceptance at the center, the school social worker wishes to present a formal family history.

> C. [Important to involve nursery school staff immediately and not let them be pushed into the background by all this "brass."]
> *First, let's hear a description of the child's behavior in school and the staff's experience with her.*
> T. (Teachers describe the child's behavior. She constantly sucks anything she can get hold of and is preoccupied with turning wheels and spinning objects. She eats poorly, throws food, and won't sit on the toilet, but she will respond to cuddling by

adults and has made a tentative relationship with one little boy.)

C. [It is clear that this child functions at a grossly retarded level in many areas, and places a heavy burden on teachers in an overcrowded center not geared for this kind of problem. However, she is not completely autistic and has made some progress.]

History now presented by the social worker portrays a disturbed, guilty mother who denies that the child has serious problems. At the moment she is unmotivated for referral to a psychiatric facility and will be helped by guidance personnel.

C. [Need to precipitate expression of the staff's feeling of helplessness.]

What do you feel you would need in order to handle this case ideally?

T. Three or four psychiatrists and some psychologists!

C. [Now maybe we can get reoriented to exploring the problem.]

I can see why you feel overwhelmed! It is a very difficult case, and you may have to abandon it if it gets to be too much. However, at the moment the child seems to be making more progress than I would have anticipated.

T. Nursery school teachers are supposed to be able to do everything, but maybe we could handle it if we had a little help.

C. [Permission to reject the problem seems to have acted as a challenge.]

Would it be possible administratively to get some extra help?

Administrator discusses with teachers what kind of help they feel they need and agrees to put in an additional assistant teacher at least for the time being.

C. [Staff will need a lot of support and encouragement.]

For the next few months we'll use our consultation sessions to talk about this case whenever you wish.

Second, Third, and Fourth Monthly Sessions

For the next three months, sessions are devoted essentially to progress reports on this child. Staff members are spending much time holding or carrying her, but they express no resentment and feel that with an extra teacher the center as a whole is operating normally. The child is eating and sleeping better and has progressed a little in making relationships with her peers, although she still will not use the toilet and is still preoccupied with revolving objects.

>C. [Teachers are obviously getting satisfaction from her improvement.]
>*You are doing a good job with her.*
>Consultant answers many questions, and gives a lot of general information about autistic children.

Fifth Session

Teachers now again show obvious anxiety as they present the material. The child has begun actively pursuing both adults and children, but now she behaves so aggressively that the staff fears for the safety of other children. They again complain about the burden she imposes and are violently critical of the mother for not "doing something." They express a wish that the child could be sent to a therapeutic nursery school and repeatedly emphasize a need for "tests."

>C. [Pressure on the staff seems to result from their anxiety rather than from any real increase of difficulty in handling the child. They have regressed to a helpless attitude, at least partly because, despite all the attention paid her, the child does not seem to them to be much better.]
>*Aggression of this kind does put a load on the staff, but it is really a sign of great progress. Her improvement has*

been dramatic, and *I* doubt very much that she would have done any better in any kind of therapeutic facility.

T. It's all very well to come along and pat us on the back, but we are the ones stuck with the work.

(Teachers complain that nobody appreciates what they have been through and now protest openly against administration and consultant for not helping more.)

C. [They must be afraid they will get more children like this in the future if we think they have done so well with this one.]

You have helped turn the tide for this child at a period crucial for her, but she doesn't belong in this kind of school. Fortunately she will soon be gone, and you won't have such a problem again.

T. (Staff immediately begins to talk more optimistically, and by the end of the session, anxiety is greatly reduced.)

The child was not presented again for the duration of her stay, and the teachers returned to using sessions in a way they had learned to do before the consultant went away. In later years, however, they frequently referred with pride to the fact that they had been able to help this child, and were gratified to hear that she maintained her gains and eventually made a marginal adjustment to an ordinary public school in the new community.

Center C is in a marginal section of town, where more than half the families are from minority groups and many receive welfare aid. The head teacher has had minimal formal professional training but has had many years experience and is motherly, with a natural gift for handling children and relating to parents. She directs the nursery school program rather formally, through a hierarchical chain of command. Assistant teachers are young, were educated in modern training centers, and are somewhat resentful of this approach; but most are of a personality type well suited to a somewhat rigidly structured setting. One or two unusually gifted individuals are personally threatened by what they consider to be the "authoritarianism." Physical facilities both indoors and out are completely inadequate for the number of children served.

In-service training sessions have always been highly structured, with staff members sitting around a table according to rank. The head teacher calls on each teacher in turn for comment, and if the consultant asks for comments from the group, they also speak in turn after looking to the head teacher for permission.

First Session after Consultant's Absence

    T. (A formal welcome is made by the head teacher who then asks another teacher to present a case. Case presentation: A welfare agency referred to the center two children whose mother is considered incompetent to care for them during the day. The younger sister is much brighter than her three-year-old brother, the main subject of discussion. Is he mentally retarded, and if so, how should he be handled in school?)

    C. [This group has also regressed to making demands for diagnosis and direct suggestions instead of exploring the problem for themselves. They need reorientation to seeking their own solutions.]

    What is the boy's observable behavior?

    T. (Teachers describe it and in the course of discussion come to a rapid conclusion that if he were treated like a two-year-old, there would be no problem. They themselves make suggestions for a change in his program.)

    C. [The teachers obviously know how to handle this boy. Why are they presenting him? Does some stereotype about mental retardation get in their way, or are they presenting some underlying problem via the case?]

What aspect of the problem would you like to explore further?

Head T. Can the *mother* be helped?

C *What does she seem to want?*

Head T. Comfort and support.

Asst. 1. She can't give the children much.

Asst. 2. She's more interested in getting support for herself.

Asst. 3. We can't expect much from her. We'll have to wait till she leaves and then do whatever we think is best.

Asst. 4. Even though we recognize the problem, what can we do to make him *behave?*

C. [Head teacher and staff are discussing their own feelings about relationships at the center.]

You have answered all your own questions, and in spite of your doubts have handled the child according to his mental age. If you keep relying on your own observations, you won't have to worry about diagnostic labels.

Second Session, One Month Later

T. (Case presentation: A four-year-old boy who has been in school for several months has malformation of the eyes and very poor vision, verbalizes poorly, and seems retarded. The teachers describe his behavior as that of a much younger child, but he is large and strong, reminding them of Lennie in *Of Mice and Men*. He seems affectionate and good-natured but constantly hits and pushes smaller children. Calls all teachers "Mommy" and often tries to kiss them on the eyes. It turns out later that his mother does this to him.)

C. [They have set up a clear-cut stereotype. Focus on that.]

Let's all tell how we reacted to Lennie in the book.

T. (All members of the group except one picture a dumb, affectionate creature who didn't know his own strength. One says she felt some revulsion toward him and then admits that she feels repelled when this child tries to kiss her eyes.)

Consultant says that to her Lennie portrayed a picture of masked aggression arising from frustration, and that because of this she has been assuming throughout this discussion that the child's kisses are a form of assault. She then uses the whole discussion to illustrate how the presence of a stereotype can cause everyone to see in a child qualities he may not possess or to miss things that may not fit the stereotype.

Group then reexamines the child's actual behavior and concludes that he does give evidence of frustration. They discuss how the school routine could be varied to meet his needs better.

(Although the number of retarded children in this center was not greater than in others, more than half of the cases presented over a four-year period had something to do with retardation.)

In an earlier theoretical section, stress was laid upon the idea that, when dealing with in-service training groups, a psychiatric consultant must exercise the same basic attitudes and therapeutic skills that he employs in individual or group psychotherapy, but that he must focus his activities on a different kind of objective. Just as in therapy, he must be able to evaluate sources of individual or group anxiety and meet the emotional needs of those with whom he is dealing professionally. As in therapy, or as in the supervision of a therapist (Ekstein and Wallerstein, 1958), he must be able to recognize that choice and handling of material presented for discussion may reflect underlying personal or group conflicts and that the presenting problem frequently is not the real problem for which help is sought.

On the other hand, as leader of in-service training, he no longer operates within the explicit or implicit contract to uncover sources of intrapsychic conflict in the workers and must focus only on those factors which distort perception or otherwise interfere with the objectivity required to carry out a specific professional task. An important aspect of the consultant's job with in-service training groups is to estimate the morale and climate of any group. He may encourage open discussion of emotional reactions which cause difficulty only when he feels in the group a specific readiness to tolerate this kind of discussion. Knowledge about special problems of the group is an important factor in his ability to make such a judgment.

The descriptions of sessions at Centers A and C demonstrate that even when a consultant is aware that a group is presenting its own problem through cases chosen for presentation, knowledge of the particular character of an individual agency and the personalities within it influences his choice of whether or not to uncover the underlying problem.

At Center A, the group unconsciously chose to express its own anxiety about abandonment by the consultant by presenting cases with which they were in some way identified. Teachers' perceptions of professional problems were distorted by intrusion of their own reaction. The consultant's knowledge of the group indicated that discussion of their own feelings would at some time be appropriate, but awareness that timing was not right in the first session after absence required that focus remain on the client. By the second session, when teachers again presented a child who was not really giving trouble but seemed to represent symbolically their own wish to progress faster in achieving independence, a climate of acceptance had been reestablished and the consultant could "interpret from the side of the ego" to precipitate release of the anger, restore perspective in the group, and permit its members to abandon their overcompensatory glorification of the consultant's power. In future sessions, members of the group spontaneously explored their own feelings about every child who seemed to present a problem and freely discussed their reactions to problems faced by all nursery school teachers.

At Center C the situation was entirely different. Although previous knowledge of the center's problems, staff comments about the first case presented, and subsequent emphasis on selection of cases involving retardation all suggested to the consultant that this group too was expressing personal feelings about being "held back," open discussion of the underlying problem was out of the question at all times. An uncovering of the source for staff anxiety would have produced a complete breakdown of morale at Center C. The climate at this school required that consultant activity be limited to supplying factual information and helping the group develop techniques for finding their own solutions to practical problems. Distortions in perception could to some extent be corrected if the consultant actively concentrated on preserving the self-esteem of all group members. Use of her own reaction to illustrate the effect of a stereotype is an example of one such measure. Acceptance and reassurance by the consultant could reduce staff tension over the handling of specific problems, but the subject of interactions among personnel at this center could not be touched through a 10-year period of in-service training.

Sessions at Centers A and B illustrate the concept that although some attitudes expressed by agency personnel indicate that intrapsychic conflicts may exist in certain staff members, such conflicts remain outside the realm of subject matter considered appropriate for exploration by an in-service training group. The personal sources for prestige need reflected by anxiety over loss of a consultant at Center A, or of the competitiveness shown by staff members at both centers in an overcompensatory glorification of therapists were never touched, even when, at Center A, the group could openly acknowledge narcissistic gratification from having a consultant.

Sessions at Center B also illustrate that a consultant to in-service training programs must sometimes shift roles to undertake what Caplan has termed "crisis consultation" at a time of emergency. Failure to meet such a need would endanger his relationship to a group and hamper subsequent attempts to function another way.

One can see here the way in which staff education may serve a double function. The consultant's major activities during a six-month period were directed primarily toward relieving staff anxieties to a point where they could see that they were performing a therapeutically valuable service to an individual child and that this could be accomplished without much disruption of their normal roles as nursery school teachers. At the same time, the staff was given considerable education about autism in general and about the meaning of change from withdrawal to overt aggression. Since their regression to helplessness and dependent attitudes was at least in part due to ignorance of the fact that this change in the child's behavior constituted improvement in her psychic state, education became in itself a tool for bringing about reduction of tension in the group.

CHAPTER VIII

SUMMARY

In the preceding chapters I have touched on a number of theoretical and practical aspects of mental health in-service training for workers whose primary professional task is not psychotherapy but who, in carrying out their own work effectively, have a potentially psychotherapeutic effect on individuals with whom they work.

Problems facing the consultant from a psychological profession who newly assumes a role as leader of in-service training groups and the influences upon him have been discussed in some detail, with illustrations taken from my own experience. I have also presented certain observations and opinions based on acquaintance with members of these groups and the agency settings in which they operated, hoping that these ideas may serve as useful background material for members of the psychological professions newly embarking on work with similar groups from the same kinds of professions. No attempt has been made to tell how to run consultation sessions or how to handle situations mentioned in illustrations.

I have stressed the fact that no matter how great his experience as psychotherapist, the mental health consultan† who wishes to conduct in-service training must acquire new knowledge and skills and must overcome certain biases created by previous modes of functioning. However, in all the foregoing material I have also tried to demonstrate unequivocally that despite the need for changes in focus and for development of new techniques, the basic knowledge with which the consultant practices his new role is the same as that with which he carries on his own profession. I hope I have shown that clinical judgment, skill, and experience are still a psychotherapist's most effective tools for becoming an effective leader of in-service training groups.

The vital importance of clinical judgment and experience in handling group discussions of psychological material, emotionally charged for many, is a prime reason for recommending that mental health in-service training programs be conducted by individuals with specific *clinical* training in the psychological professions. I feel it necessary to place strong final emphasis upon this point because in view of a shortage in trained personnel, leaders in the community psychiatry movement are at present encouraging the use of clinically untrained group leaders in many capacities. Sometimes they are useful but at other times inadequately controlled and hazardous. There is a trend in this country toward forming various kinds of groups intended to be therapeutic by allowing free expression of feelings among those attending. Most clinicians are aware of the dangers inherent in precipitate attack on psychic defenses, but some group leaders seem insufficiently aware of the need for training in the ability to anticipate and handle untoward reactions that may occur among participants.

When groups are avowedly constructed for "group therapy," an explicit contract to explore personal reactions has at least been established at the outset among participants operating with or without trained leaders. However, even such groups may be hazardous when they involve people who must work together closely on their jobs. Today there is a trend in some schools toward setting up a form of group therapy known as "sensitivity training" which faculty members are encouraged to attend. In areas where this is occurring, quite a few teachers are coming to psychiatrists of the community in various kinds of panic states brought on by a need to expose personal problems and anxieties to their colleagues. Recently, also, other types of groups have begun to be set up in some schools and agencies, supported by federal or local government grants and led by persons who are not clinically oriented, such as health educators or school teachers with only academic backgrounds for "counseling" (sometimes with a little experience in personal psychotherapy to increase their confidence in psychological sophistication). Such groups, structured to encourage free interchange of ideas and feelings among clients and staff members, are intended to produce a more "swinging" faculty or staff, in tune with the mood of today's young people. Unfortunately, while the goal may be worthy, such a method is at times highly dangerous to the mental health of some exposed individuals.

I should like to close this book with a warning that group work of this kind should not be confused with mental health in-service training groups scientifically conducted by trained clinicians.

REFERENCES

Caplan, G. (1964), *Principles of Preventive Psychiatry*. New York: Basic Books.
Ekstein, R., and Wallerstein, R. S. (1958), *The Teaching and Learning of Psychotherapy*. New York: Basic Books.
Ginsberg, E. L. (1950), *Public Health is People*. New York: Commonwealth Fund.
Lemkau, P. V. (1949), *Mental Hygiene in Public Health*. New York: McGraw-Hill.
Parker, B. (1958), Psychiatric Consultation for Non-psychiatric Professional Workers. U.S. Dept. of Health, Education & Welfare. Public Health Monograph no. 53.
———— (1961), The Value of Supervision in Training Psychiatrists for Mental Health Consultation. *Ment. Hyg.*, 45(1): 94-100.
———— (1962), Some Observations on Psychiatric Consultation with Nursery School Teachers. *Ment. Hyg.*, 46(4):559-566.
———— (1965), The Role of a Specific Father-child Interaction Pattern in the Genesis and Psychoanalytic Treatment of Obsessional Character Neurosis. *Internat. J. Psychoanal.*, 46(3):332-341.
Spiro, M. E. (1958), *Children of the Kibbutz*. Cambridge, Mass.: Harvard University Press.